MURDER

MOST FOUL

BY NICK VAN DER LEEK

"She was a great mom." — Cheryl Berreth, November 1st, 2019

"I'm not the monster they say I am." — Words attributed to Patrick Frazee by a jailhouse snitch

"…A thousand may well be stopped by three: Now, who will stand on either hand and keep the bridge with me?" — Horatius at the Bridge by Thomas Babington Macaulay

Important Note to the Reader:

The *Rocket Science* books are unique. Throughout this book, the author has provided hyperlinks to relevant resources including documents, photographs and videos to enhance your interactivity with the story.

Disclaimer:

On Monday, November 18, 2019, four days short of the one-year anniversary of Kelsey Berreth's murder, Patrick Frazee was found guilty on all eight charges brought against him in the Teller County court in Cripple Creek. These included first-degree murder, tampering with a deceased body and three counts of solicitation to commit murder. On November 18, Patrick Frazee was sentenced to life in prison without parole plus 156 years for the murder of the mother of his young child. Throughout the period when Frazee plotted his fiancé's murder, Frazee shared his strategy with friends and others in the farming community around Florissant.

"No body, no crime, right?"

TABLE OF CONTENTS

Introduction

Three days after Chris Watts was sentenced to life in a dark hole, 29-year-old Kelsey Berreth disappeared. It was as if Kelsey's killer had watched the Silver Fox sitting in court in the orange jump suit and sniggered at his television.

Dumb bastard.
I'll show you fools how...

If Chris Watts did a bad job disposing of his wife's remains, someone thought they could do better, *and they did.*

If Chris Watts did a bad job of explaining his wife's disappearance, someone thought they could do better, *and they did.* But even with the intertextual benefit of the Chris Watts case available in the airwaves to anyone who was listening – providing ongoing insight and guidance on what not to do what not to say and how not to act – committing the perfect murder <u>130 miles due south of Frederick</u> in Cripple Creek proved to be tricky.

If the Watts case provided a cautionary tale floating in the ether, and if it seemed a very easy set of circumstances to "improve" on in terms of execution, leaving digital breadcrumbs turned out to be a stickier assignment than Kelsey's killer had anticipated. It would be especially fiddly not to leave traces he didn't want to leave, while leaving traces he did want. And as the days following Kelsey's disappearance ticked by, and the Chris Watts discovery started ringing in everyone's ears – loud and clear – someone started feeling a chilling unease creeping up on him, on them.

Dumb bastard.
I'll show you fools how…
Maybe not so dumb after all…

After a quick review of the discovery in late November, early December, they realized they might not have thought about *everything* after all.

The hardest thing in true crime is getting rid of the body *without leaving any traces*. Almost as hard is committing a crime without being seen – whether by human eyes, digital sensors or through the olfactory skills of trained K9 units. The shadow of realization slowly stole upon Kelsey's killer. As it did, the investigators in Teller County seemed to rise from a stupor. Kelsey wasn't missing. Foul deeds had awoken somewhere across the fields and fells of Cripple County.

Cast of Characters

"People go missing all the time." — Patrick Frazee

Berreth Family

1. Kelsey. Flight instructor at Doss Aviation [part-time] in Pueblo. Resident in Woodland Park. Seventh Day Adventist. Disappeared midday, November 22nd from her home under mysterious circumstances. Reported missing December 2nd. Presumed deceased.

2. Kaylee, born on October 5th, 2017. Kaylee was 1 year and approximately 1 month old when her mother was beaten to death by her own father. Kaylee was present in the home during the incident. Subject of ongoing custody dispute between her engaged but separated parents in the run-up to Kelsey's brutal murder.

3. <u>Cheryl Berreth</u>, victim's mother. Testified on Trial Day 1 and Trial Day 2.

4. Darrell Berreth, victim's father. Apparently tried to make eye contact with Frazee on Trial Day 9, but Frazee avoided his gaze. Cheryl didn't attend court after finishing her testimony. Darrell sat through it until the end.

5. <u>Clint Berreth</u>, victim's brother. Testified on Trial Day 2.

6. <u>Brandon Kimble</u>, Clint's partner.

7. JoDee Garretson. Kelsey's cousin. Appeared in a Dateline documentary about Kelsey.

Berreth Neighbors and Related

1. Leslie Jackson. Neighbor. Jackson's residence was equipped with Arlo surveillance cameras. <u>Footage from a camera directed towards Jackson's bedroom window</u>, but picking up Kelsey's front door, was used extensively during the criminal trial.

2. Angela Gerber. Elderly neighbor who gave Kelsey a baby gate. Properties share a wall. Testified on Trial Day 2. Gerber was in Utah for Thanksgiving.

3. Sue Gorney. Previous home owner. Testified on Trial Day 9 about floorboards, and that she cut herself when she moved out of the residence.

4. Kate Loucado. Former co-worker.

Doss Aviation

1. Raymond Siebring. Owner of Doss Aviation. Testified on Trial Day 2. Siebring described Kelsey as "incredibly diligent."

2. Carolyn Sharp. Flight instructor. Worked alongside Kelsey when Kelsey joined Doss Aviation. Testified on Trial Day 9. Described Kelsey as quiet and reserved.

3. Jennifer Barks. Human resources team at Doss Aviation. Barks was tasked with finding out where the AWOL Doss Aviation employee was. Testified on Trial Day 9.

4. Melissa Russ. Human resources business partner to Barks.

5. Robert Hill, Flight instructor. Testified on Trial Day 9 about Kelsey mentioning "a random lady" who arrived at her house with Starbucks coffee [a reference to Kenney].

Frazee Family

1. Patrick Frazee, 33-year-old <u>rancher from Florissant</u>, Colorado. Accused of murdering his 29-year-old fiancé. Also accused of tampering with a dead body and three counts of solicitation.

2. Sheila Kathleen Ryan Frazee, Patrick's mother. Former nurse. <u>Sheila was briefly detained at the time of her son's arrest</u> but not charged.

3 Robert Edwin Frazee. Formerly US Air Force. Deceased August 28th, 2019.

4. Sean Frazee, Patrick's estranged brother [estranged since 2015/2016] and police officer at Colorado Springs. Sean testified for the prosecution about seeing his brother on November 22nd at his mother's home. Frazee arrived late with his 1-year-old daughter Kaylee, at approximately 16:30, two hours after his brother arrived.

5. Erin Frazee, from Larkspur Colorado.

6. Pamela Flowers. Partner of Erin Frazee.

Frazee Ranch

1. Two eighteen-year-old ranch hands assisted Frazee in covering up a burn patch with dirt.

Frazee Friends and Acquaintances

1. Savannah Greasby. Nurse. Based in Colorado Springs. Greasby exchanged flirtatious texts with Frazee the day before he allegedly murdered Kelsey, and subsequent to the incident. Testified on Trial Day 7.

2. Vanessa Curie. Ex-girlfriend. Frazee dated Curie for three years. <u>Incarcerated at the Denver Women's Correctional Facility</u> on misdemeanour charges relating to burglary, probation violation, criminal mischief and drug-related incidents

3. Robert Slagle. Frazee's best friend for ten years. Testified on Trial Day 7. Slagle went to Kelsey's home at Frazee's request, ostensibly to collect "alibi evidence." Part of this alibi was Frazee going over a timeline several times, and writing it on an envelope for Slagle to remember. Testified on Trial Day 7.

4. Laurie Luce. Frazee trimmed her horses' hooves. Frazee told Luce Kelsey was "unstable" and didn't want to be a mother. Luce testified on Trial Day 7.

5. Joseph Moore [thought of Frazee as a stepson]. Moore said Frazee had told him in April 2018, 'No body, no crime.' Moore was with Frazee at Five Guys when the FBI arrived and confiscated his phone. At the time <u>Frazee assured Moore he had called a number in Idaho 'to talk about horses.'</u>

6. Katherine Donahue. Canon City. Testified on Trial Day 7 that Frazee never had anything good to say about Kelsey.

7. Kayla Daugherty. Dated Frazee in the spring of 2016.

8. Tim Graf, co-owner of Blue Mountain Ranch youth summer camp in Florissant. Graf and Frazee graduated in the same class

at Woodland Park High School in 2004.

9. Gilda Dellinger. Friend of Frazee for 20 years who described Frazee as "kind and helpful" in January 2019.

10. Clinton Cline, president of Two Mile High Club in Cripple Creek, a non-profit custodian of the local, itinerant donkey herd. Cline blamed the media for portraying Frazee "incorrectly" as a bad guy. Cline also characterized Frazee as Kaylee's primary caretaker and custodian.

11. Dana Souligny. Wrote an endorsement on Facebook that her son's girlfriend grew up with Frazee, and that he was "a great guy."

12. Sonja Oliver. Friend of five years. Described Frazee on December 18th, 2018 as "a gentle soul."

13. Jacob Bentley. Jailhouse snitch. Testified on Trial Day 10 about 17 notes Frazee allegedly wrote to him, asking him to murder several witnesses, including Kenney and FBI Agent Gregg Slater.

Kenney Family

1. Krystal Lee Kenney, 32. Originally from Hansen, Idaho. Subsequently resident in Kimberly, eight miles from Twin Falls [near to where Kelsey's phone pinged in Gooding on November 25th]. Nurse. Former Idaho High School Rodeo Queen, long time mistress of Patrick Frazee and alleged [confessed] accomplice. Kenney took a plea deal in exchange for her testimony. Kenney's intent in terms of the crime appears to be that she wanted to "impair" the police investigation into her long-time lover.

2. Sidney Dustin Kenney, Krystal's father. Provided alibi and described her in court as a 'people pleaser.'

3. Chad Lee. Ex-husband. He told FBI Agent Rodney Draper that Kenney had bought a new phone on December 17th, 2018.

Kenney Friends and Acquaintances

1. Megan Garrison. Swapped vehicles with Kenney when Kenney drove down to Colorado to clean up the crime scene. Garrison's vehicle is a black Volkswagen <u>Passat sedan</u>. A loaded gun was found under the seat. <u>Kenney and Garrison exchanged vehicles at a Walmart in Idaho</u>.

2. Dru Nielsen. Kenney's attorney. Indicated on December 2nd <u>the intent to file a motion that Kenney's actions were not "aggravated"</u> in terms of her involvement in Kelsey's death.

3. Delynn Bird. Previously worked with Kenney in the recovery room at St. Luke's Magic Valley Hospital.

4. Allyson Wright. Previously worked with Kenney in the recovery room at St. Luke's Magic Valley Hospital. Wright filled in for Kenney's shift on November 24th, 2018. Wright said Kenney had said she needed to do "something" in Colorado, without specifying what exactly.

5. Abbey Abbondandolothe. Senior director of security. Testified on Trial Day 6 that Kenney was at work on November 21st and November 23rd.

FBI

1. FBI Special Agent Charles DeFrance [tested Kelsey's home for blood traces].

2. Special Agent Rodney Draper. Testified on Day 7.

CBI

1. Gregg Slater. Testified several times, including on Trial Day 9 and 10. Slater interviewed Krystal Kenney on December 17th, 2018. Slater testified that he didn't know where the investigation would be without Krystal Kenney's cooperation.

2. Jerry Means. Fire Investigator. Testified on Trial Day 7.

3. Tanya Atkinson, Crime Scene Analyst [CSA]. Testified on Trial Day 7. Atkinson photographed and processed the scene at Kelsey's apartment [February 2019] and at the Nash Ranch [December 21st, 2018]. Atkinson found "wipe marks" in several areas of Kelsey's apartment, leading her to believe it had been cleaned.

4. Eric Bryant, CSA. Testified on Trial Day 7. Bryant tested deposits and discolorations on the hay bale on the Nash Ranch.

5. Caitlin Rogers, DNA analyst. Testified on Trial Day 9 about not being able to positively identify stains on the hay bale as blood.

6. Michael Hecht. Interviewed several of Kelsey's co-workers at Doss Aviation. Testified on Trial Day 9.

7. Chief Jerry Means [ex-CBI]. Adams County Fire Rescue Investigations. 30 years' experience. Testified on Trial Day 7.

Law Enforcement and Related

1. Greg Couch, Teller County Sheriff Commander.

2. Chris Paulsen. Teller County Sheriff's deputy. Works on FBI Task Force.

3. Lee Richards, 4th Judicial District Attorney's Office spokeswoman.

4. <u>Mary Longmire</u>, case worker for the Department of Human Services. Testified on Trial Day 9.

5. Josh Hayes. Twin Falls detective. Obtained warrant to search Kenny's home [from her ex-husband] on December 17th, and December 21st, 2018.

6. Stephanie Courtney. District Attorney's Office Investigator. Courtney tracked down Frazee's movements via Walmart surveillance video and ATM surveillance video. Testified on Trial Day 3.

7. Dr. Diane France. Forensic anthropologist. Testified on Trial Day 9.

8. Jonathyn Priest. Crime scene analyst. Retired 30-year police officer. Priest reconstructed the crime scene. Testified on Trial Day 10 that Kelsey was likely clubbed 10-15 times, each blow made with extreme force.

Woodland Park Police Department

1. Police Chief Miles De Young.

2. Corporal Beth Huber. Huber joined the investigation on December 3rd. Prosecutor Beth Reed interviewed her on the stand on Trial Day 3.

3. Corporal Dena Currin. Responded to Cheryl Berreth's request for a welfare check on December 2nd.

4. Andrew Leibbrand. Sergeant. Accompanied Dena Currin on welfare check on December 2nd. Used a lock bypass tool to open the front door.

5. <u>Commander Christopher Adams</u>. Adams authored Krystal Kenney's affidavit.

Judges

1. Judge Linda Margaret Billings Vela. Presided over <u>preliminary hearings in late January 2019</u>.

2. Teller County District Court Judge Scott Sells. Presided over criminal murder trial in early to mid-November 2019.

Prosecution Team

1. Fourth Judicial <u>District Attorney Dan May</u>.

2. <u>Lead Prosecutor Jennifer Viehman</u>.

3. Beth Reed.

Defense Team

1. Adam Steigerwald. Public defender.

2. Ashley Porter. Public defender.

3. Jeremy Loew. Criminal Defense Lawyer. Dismissed late 2018/ early 2019.

Other Attorneys

1. Joshua Tolini. Sheila Frazee's lawyer, based in Colorado Springs.

Canine Units

1. Brian Eberle, Lucy's handler. Lucy alerted to blood traces on the bumper of Kelsey's vehicle.

2. Frank Hurst, Radar's handler. The bloodhound searched a barn on February 13 and alerted to black stains on the top of a bale of hay.

Miscellaneous Trial Witnesses

1. Patricia Key. Credit Union Manager. Frazee approached her on December 5th asking for surveillance photos of him visiting the ATM on November 22nd.

2. David Felis. Woodland Park Verizon Store employee. Testified that Frazee arrived at the store at 16:00 on December 11th appearing paranoid. Frazee told Felis: "Don't believe what they're saying about me." Frazee was concerned about third parties gaining access to his cell phone and wanted to change his PIN code. When he discovered he could not, Frazee appeared visibly shaken, according to Felis.

3. Jason Memmer. Sales and delivery employee at Williams Furniture in Woodland Park. Testified on <u>Trial Day 3</u> about Frazee's vehicle heading north – towards Kelsey's home – at 12:30. Another video showed him heading back at 12:38. This video showed a white dog carrier and black tote box in the back of his truck.

4. Shannon Kadiuraus. Woodland Park Sonic Drive In manager. Testified on Trial Day 6.

5. William David Stover. IT manager for the Florissant Conoco at 2636 W. Highway 24. Stover testified about the footage from the CCTV cameras captured on Trial Day 6.

Media

1. Sam Kraemer. Appeared on *Dateline*.

2. Ashley Franco. Appeared on *CBS*.

Social Media

1. <u>DadwithaPhone</u>.

THE PROSECUTION

"I learned Patrick Frazee had committed a homicide." — Krystal Kenney, choking back tears while reading from a handwritten statement

Issues of Identity

"I don't know that we've been on bad terms, we just haven't been close." — <u>Sean Frazee</u>, Patrick Frazee's brother

In a similar vein to the Chris Watts case, with Patrick Frazee we're less interested in matters of guilt, and more interested in matters of identity. How are Watts and Frazee different animals? How are they the same? And the same question with reference to their mistresses: how is Kessinger different to Kenney? Once we've navigated the psychological fabric of identity, we may fathom a cogent narrative beyond simplistic issues like custody.

We can also compare the Watts family to the Frazee family. How was Shan'ann different to Kelsey? How were the Watts children different to Kaylee? Why was Kaylee a survivor in this tragedy, when Bella, Ceecee and Niko were not? What was the impact of the mothers in this story – Cheryl [the counterpart to Sandi Rzucek] and Sheila [the counterpart to Cindy Watts]?

If we're going to attempt to answer these question, we should start at the beginning – with the monster at the epicentre of this heinous, immeasurable crime – Patrick Frazee.

When Frazee returned to the ranch, enervated from his handiwork, he – according to Kenney – found it hard to eat Thanksgiving dinner…

It's hard to eat Thanksgiving dinner with my family when the mother of my child is in a tote in the back of my truck…

What was harder? Trying to eat dinner or committing the murder? He told Kenney he *swung away* at Kelsey, the terms suggesting both the forcefulness of the blows and the repetition. He described what he did as *inhumane* to Kenney, a bizarrely frank concession. He added that in future he would stick to normal weapons. This suggested that he planned to repeat the same offence, but improve on his execution.

Frazee brought the tote in from the back of the truck [it's not clear what "in" refers to, but presumably inside his ranch home] after he killed Kelsey – according to Kenney. He put the baseball bat inside [again, presumably somewhere inside the home] then washed his trousers and tried to clean the rest of himself up.

Much is revealed in this simple anecdote, but before we decipher it, let's drift away from Thanksgiving, and try to find our way to a broader perspective on Frazee.

<u>Worth playing for?</u>

Who was he?

Patrick Frazee was a man in serious debt through the summer of 2018. His child support payments to Kelsey were in the order of $700 per month. They'd started in October 2017 when Kaylee was born. Less than a year later, in June [according to some reports[1]], the child

---

1 *The Daily Beast* and the <u>*Gazette* refer to child support payments end-</u><u>ing in June</u> while other sources such as <u>*9News*</u> and <u>*The Denver Channel*</u>

support payments had dried up. By December, just over a week after Kelsey's murder, Frazee defaulted on a $72 000 loan. A certified letter [dated December 5th] from the Farm Credit Bureau detailed Frazee's loan, and indicated he was in default for a payment due on December 1st, 2018.

Meanwhile, on August 9th, between one and two months following the abrupt end to Frazee's child support payments, Kaylee's father had signed a preliminary document with his attorney indicating his intention to take custody of Kaylee. Given Frazee's precarious financial situation, one wonders why Frazee would want custody. Wouldn't it be cheaper to let Kelsey maintain their daughter? Or did Frazee simply love Kaylee so much?[2]

Now, in the series of videos TCRS has provided on YouTube covering the criminal trial, one of the least watched – the most overlooked – is the video titled *Financial Mess*, dealing with Trial Day 3. It's understandable. The finances, in particular the financial *messes* of others, are of scant interest to us.[3] Would it be fair to say the financial narrative is the *least* sexy aspect of true crime?

---

refer to July as the final payment. It may be that June was the final full payment of child support, while in July Frazee's final payment fell $100 short. There is consensus that after July there were no further child support payments, in other words, no support in August, September, October or November 2018.

2 Frazee's relationship with Kaylee is an "unknown" haunting this case. This aspect was not addressed in much detail [or arguably *any* detail] at trial, which may be because Frazee himself never testified, nor anyone close to him, on his behalf.

3 Although educated in law, economics and more difficult subjects including statistics, physics and financial gearing, I must admit to finding accounting

Unfortunately, <u>the money situation in this case</u> cuts to the heart not only of Frazee himself, but the motive for this crime. On November 5th, 2018, <u>*KOAA*</u> presciently referred to *"struggling finances as a key player in this case"*, and it is, just as it was in the Watts case. Our dismissiveness of other's finances misses the point that finances [our own] are of <u>terrific</u> import to us. It should be made explicit that although Frazee seemed very eager to gain custody of Kaylee, what's less clear is *why* he wanted custody? The financial malaise provides a clue. But what is it exactly?

What was it?

Are you sure you want to hear this?

During the summer of 2018, a family feud – already in play – escalated over the estate of the Frazee patriarch following his death. Isn't it interesting that Frazee's father Robert Edwin died on August 28th, and earlier that same month Frazee had not only run out of cash for child support, but was initiating a petition for custody.[4] The former US Air Force veteran had left behind a pot of gold worth $400 000 for his offspring to squabble over, and squabble over it they did. At the time or writing, they *still are* [according to <u>*KOAA*</u>]. We will deal with the portent of this disputed inheritance, and the squabbling of the siblings around it, but for now it's sufficient to note that Frazee being completely broke just prior to his father's death, and leading up to Kelsey's murder, plays heavily into the dynamics driving this particular case.

It raises the inevitable question:

---

the most baffling of all. Not because it's difficult, *per se*, but tedious. I found it mind numbingly dull at university, and as such, never passed the exams at university level.

4 The petition was signed but never filed.

Was money a bigger factor in the Frazee case or the Watts case?

Going backwards in time to Kaylee's birth in October 2017, another obvious question arises. Why, when Kaylee was born, didn't the young couple live together? This aspect, above all, is a defining factor of this case. Kelsey was with Frazee, with him enough to bear him a little girl, and yet they weren't living together? Why not? Well, doesn't the answer to that have something to do with the other "key factor"?

...struggling finances as a key player in this case...

Doesn't the one <u>key factor</u> have something to with the <u>defining factor</u>? Is there some sort of equation, some transactionality? To test this hypothesis, what happens when we turn back the clock nine years?

As early as December 2008, a decade prior to Kelsey's murder, Frazee found out Krystal Kenney – his former girlfriend – had started dating another rancher called Chad Lee. <u>Frazee offered her a Border Collie puppy</u>. It wasn't just a gift, it was a reminder. It was his way of keeping her interested, keeping a hook in her. <u>Kenney accepted the dog</u> but a few months later, sometime in 2009, Frazee asked Kenney for a check – for the puppy. When Kenney didn't send the check **Frazee threatened to come to Idaho and kill the dog.**

In 2010 Kenney got engaged to Chad Lee but the unkilled Collie remained, barking inside the Lee home, its barks harkening Kenney back to another rancher and daydreams of another life. Each time the dog's nails clicked across the floor of the house unbidden memories knocked on the door of her subconscious, memories that would come flooding back when the time was right.

See how the money side can have murderous undertones? *Any* person pushed hard enough, and far enough by the debt burden can eventually find themselves in circumstances spiralling seemingly beyond their control. From there it's a short road to becoming desperate, and at the very end of that road is a ghost town called Despicable. The residents of Despicable are without exception losers and misfits, all despicable in their own way, whether Silver Foxes, cowboys or washed up rodeo queens. And what they all have in common is simple meat-and-potatoes moneylessness. Because of that they see themselves the way the world sees them – as despicable nobodies.

Was money a bigger factor in the Frazee case or the Watts case?

TCRS would say the real question shouldn't be a matter of which case had the bigger financial burden, but that the financial burden in both was immense, and an immensely significant aspect driving the psychological mechanism.

Although the fiscal dimension sketches at least the beginnings of an outline for who Frazee was in 2018, this silhouette is nowhere near sufficient to figuring out his psychology, and how that played into his eventual criminal intent. We will revisit this issue of financial burden throughout this narrative, what it means, and what it says about this *other side* to Frazee, but before we get to that, let's examine Kelsey.

Who was she?

When the seasoned, silver-blonde prosecutor stood up to call her first witness, Jennifer Viehman started with Kelsey's upbringing. Through her mother's voice we heard about <u>Kelsey's life on a farm</u>, and an early interest in aviation. If our impression of Kelsey is of a modern Amelia Earhart, the similarity doesn't end there. Like Earhart, Kelsey was an aviator fated to disappear off the map of the world without a trace. Well, almost. Unlike Earhart, there were traces, it just required turning over a lot of stones to find them.

We see through the trial narrative that Viehman's strategy is to introduce to the jury Kelsey as a human being. <u>Someone with a backstory</u>. Someone with dreams of flying machines.

Ironically on Trial Day 1 [dealt with in the next chapter], the defense sought to dismantle the prosecution's version of things by offering the jury the idea of an inverted fairy tale. They described the prosecution's case as a beautiful house with serious foundation issues. It wasn't clear whether this slur was aimed solely at the prosecution, or whether it could be applied in some way to Kelsey. What is clear is that it could be applied to Frazee.

...a beautiful house with serious foundation issues...

Frazee presented an attractive front. The handsome rancher. But something unseen [his true financial situation] was a rotten secret buried out of sight, eating at the foundations of that face, that façade, like a fungus.

In comparison to Frazee, his finances in particular, Kelsey looked to be in good shape. She had a decent job as a flight instructor at Doss Aviation, a company that provides flight training for the military as well as international armed services. The company took care of Kaylee's medical insurance, and Frazee was initially listed as a beneficiary on Kelsey's life insurance, until he wasn't. Taking a broad view, Kelsey had not one but two vehicles at the time of her death, and well-to-do parents. They bought her condo from Sue Gorney, the previous tenant for 26 years, for $185 000 and gave it to Kelsey.

The brown townhome was a lot like Kelsey herself. Not extravagant, down-to-earth, humble, private and situated in a quiet neck of the Woodland Park woods.[5]

...a beautiful house with serious foundation issues...

---

5 Woodland Park is surrounded by the one-million acre Pike National Forest.

Kate Loucado, a former co-worker, described Kelsey on Facebook as "a damn good pilot" who was "awestruck by a handsome rancher" who'd taken an interest in her. Kelsey and Frazee made a striking, if strange couple. If Kelsey was independent, he – the middle child – still lived with his infirm elderly mother. Clearly he was dependent on his mother for his home and livelihood, and Sheila in turn – as will be made clear – appeared to be dependent on her middle child as well. If Kelsey was sweet, shy and reserved, <u>Frazee was boisterous, loud, rude and frequently rough in his manner</u>.

Most of all, <u>as Loucado put it</u>, Kelsey was a farm girl looking for "someone with strong family values" as well as "someone who held <u>the same beliefs</u> and morals."[6]

…a beautiful house with serious foundation issues…

Frazee appeared to be that, except, as it turned out, he didn't have strong family values, nor did he hold to the same lofty beliefs or morals as she did. Furthermore, Kelsey's parents were Seventh Day Adventists [SDA], and Kelsey shared the same sense of reliability, consideration and honesty as most SDA congregants. Again, the same can't be said for Frazee in any of these respects, specifically in his ability to meet and maintain his financial obligations, to Kelsey and to the local bank.

Perhaps the best character witness for Kelsey was Raymond Siebring, the owner of Doss Aviation. Siebring testified on Trial Day 2. He described Kelsey as incredibly diligent, strong, resilient and psychologically tough. If Kelsey was no physical match for the handsome rancher, she was more than a match for him spiritually, and it's in this area that the two began to chafe at one another.

---

6 If Kelsey was an observant Christian [or Seventh Day Adventist], Patrick Frazee seemed less so.

TRIAL DAY 1:

"Calculating Manipulator"

"This is the case of a cold, calculated manipulator. This man is a killer."— Proseculor Jennifer Viehman

As criminal trials go, the Patrick Frazee trial got off to a cracking start. After seating a seven women five men jury on the morning of November 1st, a Friday, Kelsey's mother Cheryl took the stand on Friday afternoon. One week later a total of 30 witnesses had already been heard, a daily blitz averaging around six new faces each day. Given that the mistress's testimony took up virtually all of Trial Day 4, and part of Trial Day 5, the witnesses spinning through the revolving door was astonishing, and even dizzying.

Let's begin at the beginning, when Kelsey's mother took the stand.

Choosing Kelsey's mother to kick off the trial was an interesting choice. They could have started with Krystal, so why didn't they? The prosecution wanted – needed – to get off to a strong start. They needed to win the jury's confidence, as is typical in criminal trials. In a high-profile case like this, if you're a prosecutor, it's even more important to get the jury on your side from the get go. There is plenty of rumor, gossip and speculation playing in the background. The prosecution's job is to tell the more compelling story. Let me repeat that. The prosecution's job is to be a better storyteller than the defense. A compelling story tends to be a convincing one.

One reason why not to start off with Krystal, is that the grieving mother wins an instant sympathy vote from the jury. It's impossible not to be sympathetic to the murdered woman's mother, or through her, to the 29-year-old deceased young mother herself. Developing emotional rapport with the jury is a more effective way of getting the jury on their side [a jury with two more women than men, incidentally], and in spite of efforts to be rational, many juries tend to think with their hearts first, and their heads second.

If the prosecution had started with their star witness – Kenney – they may have wowed the jury with shocking evidence, but Kenney herself is a controversial, and perhaps not entirely trusted figure. After Krystal's testimony, interestingly, it was her father – not her mother – who vouched for her on the stand. In Kelsey's case, it's her mother, first and foremost, not her father,[7] who vouches for her. It will be interesting to see who vouches for Frazee, when the defense sets out their case. More than likely it will be his mother[8] – and this aspect seems to echo the same thing in the Watts case: dominant mothers and dogged, tenacious mistresses.

Curiously, when Frazee appeared at trial on Friday, his first appearance in front of a jury of his peers, he was dressed for the first time in attire other than the standard green and white banded prison county jumpsuit. Instead, the jury saw a well-dressed man in a neat blue and white striped button-down shirt. In criminal trials, it's not only emotions that matter, appearances do too.

____

7 Kelsey's brother Clint testified shortly after Cheryl did.
8 Patrick Frazee's father died in 2018.

…a beautiful house with serious foundation issues…

1: CHERYL

The <u>*New York Times* review of Cheryl Berreth's testimony</u> on Friday afternoon, November 1st, was summed up neatly in a single short paragraph.

*…Kelsey Berreth's mother testified Friday that **her daughter's relationship with the Frazee family was never good**….the family viewed [Kelsey] as a "hooker" because she would arrive at their property late at night because of her work hours [at Doss Aviation]. **The relationship worsened after Kelsey told the Frazees**[9] **about her pregnancy in the summer of 2017**[10]…*

Arguably, this brief summary of testimony from Kelsey's mother ought to suffice. Not only did Frazee's family [AKA Sheila Frazee] not approve of Kelsey, when Kelsey fell pregnant, Frazee's family [Sheila] became even more *disapproving*. While knowledge of the disapproving mother-in-law, or mother-in-law-to-be is significant, it's too simplistic without context. We need to know why "Frazee's family" were so harsh and critical towards Kelsey.

If we compare this snippet out of the Frazee story to fairy tales about disapproving mother-in-laws in general [known as witches in these folk tales], why are the princesses invariably cast out? Why was Cinderella cast out? How did Snow White end up living on her own in a forest? What's the essence of the thing eating at the witches in these stories?

---

9 Effectively "telling the Frazee family" about the pregnancy meant telling Frazee's disapproving mother Sheila.

10 Kaylee was born on October 5th, 2017.

The first clues to answering these questions filter down through the backstory, provided by Cheryl, for how Kelsey came to be in Colorado in the first place. She moved to Colorado for love, after meeting Frazee online[11] in "early 2016".[12] This move happened in May 2016, which means the couple could only have known one another five months maximum, before Kelsey packed up her life to be with the new man in her life.

As it turned out, Cheryl and Kelsey's father helped Kelsey and Frazee pack for her trip – ostensibly for a new life – on the prairie outside a quaint sounding place called Cripple Creek.

According to *The Denver Channel*:

Frazee, Berreth and her parents loaded a trailer with her possessions and the couple drove from Warden Washington to Florissant, Colorado. [13] *Frazee had purchased Berreth a studio [apartment] where she lived when she first moved there.* **Berreth and Frazee never lived together at any point in their relationship,** *though Berreth would often visit [Frazee's ranch] over weekends…*

---

11 Chris Watts and Shan'ann Watts also met online when Chris Watts sent Shan'ann a friend request.

12 According to Kelsey's cousin JoDee Garretson, Kelsey and Frazee met in early 2016.

13 The drive from Kelsey's home in Washington, to Frazee's home in Colorado would have taken almost 19 hours, covering a distance of over 1200 miles. Interestingly **the route to Colorado from Washington is through Idaho**, the location of Frazee's mistress and home to Kelsey's mother, and the same route Frazee alleged sent Kelsey's phone after her death to simulate her continued existence. The fact that Frazee himself drove this route would have etched the geography in his mind.

Consider the irony: Shortly after falling in love Kelsey moves halfway across America to be with her beau, only to live *apart*[14] from him…because…why?

She's moved out of state, over 1200 miles to be with him only to *not* live with him.

Instead, she resigns herself to living 15 miles [20 minutes] apart. In doing so, Kelsey's parents are forced to fork out around $185 000 for her digs. It's not as if either of them can afford this purchase. He can't, and when Kelsey arrived in Colorado, she was unemployed – she couldn't. So why the unnecessary purchase? And then they're engaged. And then, despite falling pregnant in early 2017, the couple *continue not to live together*. Why?

Once again, context is important. Although we're not going to deal with Sheila Frazee in this chapter at any length [the *In Laws* chapter does that], it's worth noting that 33-year-old Frazee was living with his mother right through his dalliances with Kenney and Kelsey, and through the fateful pregnancies with both women. If Frazee seemed like a nice guy, with a nice ranch, and a nice ranch home, living with him – or trying to – was *complicated* by his still living with his mother.

This word – *complicated* – was actually used by the prosecutor in her opening statement to describe Frazee and Berreth's relationship on Trial Day 1. In fact <u>Viehman emphasized the status of the couple's</u>

---

14 Kelsey's two-bedroom apartment 15 miles from the Frazee ranch cost $184,900. It's not clear whether Kelsey purchased the apartment, or whether Frazee did, or whether it was purchased jointly. <u>According to the *Express Digest*</u> Kelsey purchased it. According to *The Denver Channel* Frazee did. *The Denver Channel* misspelled apartment *appointment,* so it's possible the error lies with them. At the time of writing I contacted the reporter from *The Denver Channel* for clarification on this point, and still await an answer.

association as "very complicated", mostly because, in spite of Kelsey having a child with Frazee in October 2017, they continued to live apart. According to *The Denver Channel* reporting on Trial Day 1:

Between the new baby, <u>commuting to Pueblo for work</u> and a new home, she was exhausted and it was "just not working well for her," Viehman said.

We've strayed from Cheryl's testimony on Trial Day 1. Let's get back to it. Viehman dealt with Kelsey's upbringing on a farm and her interest in aviation. In Colorado, Kelsey turned the latter into a career. The problem was this: Kelsey making her dream come true flying in Pueblo [an hour-long commute from Woodland Park, and 80 minutes from Florissant] was tearing her apart – from her home, her daughter and her ranch romance.

We can see why Frazee appealed to Kelsey. Her upbringing on a farm meant Frazee checked some of the right boxes from her childhood. But we can also see why him being on the ranch, and tied to it, was incompatible with Kelsey's job in Pueblo. Of all the occupations out there, a rancher is one of those who needs to be on the ranch as a matter of course. So Kelsey getting a job in Pueblo was never going to work out. On the other hand, living with Frazee on the ranch wasn't going to work out either. This aspect brings us back to the summary outlined above from the *New York Times*.

Kelsey's relationship with the Frazee family was never good....
the family viewed [Kelsey] as a "hooker" because she would
arrive at their property late at night because of
her work hours...

Incredibly, according to Cheryl, this "never good" relationship with Frazee's family didn't develop over time. It was instant. In fact, on *the day Kelsey arrived on the ranch* at the end of their epic 1200 mile drive from Washington, through Idaho, and finally to her new home in Colorado, there was a huge falling out between Sheila and Kelsey. It was on this night, this first night of all nights, that Frazee's mother accused Kelsey of being a hooker. According to Sheryl, this accusation rained fire the next morning. What had happened was they had arrived at the ranch late in the evening, and the couple had decided to unpack Kelsey's belongings the following day.

According to Cheryl, Kelsey and Sheila "worked past" the ugly incident on that fateful first night, but feelings of mutual impingement "didn't go away." Kaylee's birth on October 5th <u>involved an ugly incident of its own</u>, this time from Frazee himself.

Kelsey's introduction to the other dimension of the Frazee dynamic came at a crucial time: just as she'd packed up her life. This unwelcome reception on her first night in Colorado was a warning to go back the long road she had come. It was a warning Kelsey ignored at her peril.

The Significance of 10 Days

*As she walked around the apartment, she put a
photo of Kelsey and Frazee face-down, Cheryl said.*
— <u>The Denver Channel</u>

In this chapter we're going to deal broadly and basically with a few general aspects of this case. In the next chapter dealing with Trial Day 2 we'll nail down the theory with the actual evidence.

<u>Worth playing for?</u>

The prime signatures of this case are firstly that the perpetrator and victim lived apart. Secondly, that the custody of a 13-month child was hanging in the balance at the time the crime was committed. Thirdly, and most significantly, the fact that it took 10 Days[15] for anyone to raise the alarm after Kelsey disappeared. 10 Days is a long time. If you were to disappear, how long would it take for someone – anyone – to notice?

---

15 The "D" in 10 Days is capitalized for the same reason Ransom Note in the series on JonBenét Ramsey is capitalized. It's to emphasize the idiosyncratic nature in this case of the long gap before the police were contacted. Ransom Note is capitalized because of the extraordinary nature of the Ransom Note in the Ramsey case. Not only was it a bogus note, but it distinguishes itself as the Ransom Note of ransom notes.

Why did it take 10 Days for someone to raise the alarm about Kelsey?

Why?

TCRS would say as much as the question around why it took so long matters, and ought to be answered, *the real question is whether these signatures are correlated.* Now, the signatures of living apart and Kaylee's custody *do* appear to be correlated even if contradictory. The real issue is whether the two obvious signatures are correlated to the third less obvious signature of 10 Days. If they are related, precisely *how* are these signatures correlated?

In our attempt to unravel the true scope and significance of the 10 Days Signature, let's begin by approaching this question from a distance. Let's start by navigating our way through how these signatures may be related to one another.

1. "Correlation does not imply Causation"

Broadly speaking, it holds that if the new couple were living apart for an extended period, within the context of a newcomer to the family – Kaylee – then custody had to eventually become a bone of contention. The longer the couple remained apart, the sooner the custody of the child torn between the separating parents would arise. It's inevitable. If we take the notion of the 10 Days and link it to the couple living apart, we can see Frazee immediately has a sort of precedent. The fact that he wasn't living with Kelsey meant he was off the hook in knowing where she was. In this *schema* he could conceivably not be aware of her being somewhere at one moment, and gone the next. We may say, therefore, that there is a clear correlation between the separation, which preceded the crime, and the disappearance, which was a permanent separation [just as Watts' "divorce" was actually a *permanent separation* in reality, and one he had deliberately manufactured].

We can take it further and say the separation isn't only related to the disappearance, but perhaps the cause – or part of the cause – for it. In other words, no separation no disappearance. No separation no murder. No separation no custody scenario.

The custody scenario is slightly more intricate, but what we see is custody in the most ordinary sense is about being around, isn't it? In order to care, protect, supervise, guard or manage something – in this case someone – one has to be available [present] to do it. In the *schema* of this thinking, it stands to reason if someone isn't around, that duty to care for something – in this case someone – that custody must fall, must be transferred to someone else. And so we can see how Kelsey disappearing manufactures a scenario where Kaylee then needs to be transferred to someone else. Her custody needs to be taken over because her mother isn't around, and she's not around *indefinitely*.

So the custody transfer is also indefinite, but in effect, permanent. It's no coincidence then that precisely when the crime happens, what happens? – custody transfers to Frazee. And just as Watts leaks the symbolic motive for the murder when he lies about his fictional conversation with Shan'ann immediately preceding the murders [the motive is the difficulty of divorce, issues of home ownership and ongoing obligations like child support], Frazee leaks the symbolic motive for his crime. The motive isn't custody itself, it's *related* to custody.

The 10 Days are related to the separation by the simple deniability that since Frazee was already separated from Kelsey – geographically – it would seem plausible to outsiders that he wouldn't need to know Kelsey's movements. The impression of a separation would also enhance the notion that he wouldn't be expected to know. We'll expand on what Frazee did to reinforce this ruse even further in due course, via the trial narrative.

The 10 Days are related to the custody aspect in that Frazee wants and expects both outcomes. He *wants* Kelsey to not be around so that he can take over custody without the expensive red tape involved, and he very badly wants to take over custody. For some reason Frazee believes doing it by the book won't work. Just like Watts, Frazee is under the impression if he goes through a custody battle he will lose. That's an important issue in itself. He knows he will lose, he knows it's a battle he can't win and can't afford. This is a perfect match to Watts' situation with his divorce. It was a battle Watts felt he couldn't confront, and so he confronted it as a coward would – by cheating.

Why is it that Frazee is so desperate to get custody of Kaylee?[16] It's not because he loves her or has her best interests at heart. If that were true he wouldn't wish to harm a hair on her mother's head. Instead, we know Frazee has his own interests at heart, and somehow Kaylee plays right into that.

Now we're getting somewhere. But let's move from here to deal with the significance of that gap, when Kelsey disappeared and nothing happened. What does that mean?

2. The Significance of 10 Days

It doesn't take a rocket scientist to see that Kelsey missing for 10 Days without Frazee [or Sheila Frazee] raising the alarm with the authorities seems to point to serious problems – enmity – between Frazee and Kelsey. Is that fair to say?

---

16 Even after the criminal trial was concluded, on December 5th Frazee, his mother and his sister were back in court fighting tooth and nail for custody over Kaylee.

If Frazee was a lot closer to her, not only in terms of them living together, but actually engaged to her in an authentic way, then all things being equal he should have been the first to alert authorities. And Kaylee ought to have been the trigger. When it was Kelsey's turn to take over the custody [the care] of Kaylee, and she wasn't around, the first person who should have figured this out should have been Frazee. But because he's the perpetrator *and* the person at the heart of this confluence, he's able to construct and control the narrative. Who would know best if there's something to worry about, or nothing, than the person closest to Kelsey?

It's not necessary to be more explicit on this point, is it?

Now, in the same way that Frazee not raising the alarm for 10 Days raises serious legitimate issues about the quality of his relationship with Kelsey, and the quality of his custodianship of Kaylee, it also raises questions about Kelsey's relationship with *her* family. Just as Frazee was separated from Kelsey by a few miles, Kelsey's family were separated from her by a few hundred miles. Even so, a protracted silence developed, and for whatever reason, the Berreth's didn't think it was abnormal for 10 Days.

We may be inclined to focus on Kelsey's relationship with Frazee, and *vice versa*, but there may be some reason to believe Kelsey's relationship with her family wasn't as close as it seemed. For one thing, Kelsey was telling those around her that she was married to Frazee when she wasn't. Where else could this pressure – social pressure – have originated from, than her well-to-do SDA parents? And even if Kelsey's folks were on good terms with Kelsey, they may not have been on the *best* terms as long as the untenable and frankly unethical situation of the unresolved engagement continued.

By paying for this and subsidizing that, Kelsey's parents may have meant well, but they were also exerting pressure on their daughter, albeit remotely, to make this relationship work. According to *The Denver Channel's* coverage on the topic of Kelsey and Frazee's communal financial hardship:

*Cheryl told her daughter she would help them buy a ranch, but **Frazee worried about family perception if he couldn't make a payment**. They also struggled when Kelsey was offered a pilot job in Grand Junction. **Frazee didn't want her to leave, but also wanted her to have a job,** Cheryl said. She said she remembers telling Kelsey she could use those flying hours to land a better job and that she could still go home to see Frazee on the weekends.*

From this we see Frazee was a difficult dude to please. Even when you were giving him something, he didn't like what it looked like. When Kelsey found work far afield to pick up the financial slack, he didn't seem to like what that felt like. For all his charm and cowboy good looks, he was something of a dead beat stuck in a dead beat job, on a ranch that was withering.

If it's true, if Kelsey's parents were exerting pressure from afar to get things to a point where their daughter could tie the knot, then the vibe coming from home was well-founded. Because Kelsey *did* need to sort things out – or get out. She *did* need to find a way – or be on her way. But if she received any signs or cyphers, any cautions or caveats from her parents in this respect Kelsey ignored or postponed them too, at her peril.

The Second Witness and the Invisible Crime Scene

"There's blood everywhere. There's blood on the walls. There's blood on the fireplace. There's blood on the couch. There's blood on items in the kitchen. Hobby lobby bags. Children's toys." — Jennifer Viehman, <u>opening statement to the jury</u>

On Trial Day 2 – a feathery grey, crispy cold Colorado morning, eventually burning bright blue in Cripple Creek – Cheryl continued testifying. She spoke of declining cattle prices bedevilling the lot of her daughter and her new beau. It was just bad luck. Bad luck and bad timing.

Mothers know best, they say, and <u>Cheryl Berreth said she knew *something* was amiss with Kelsey</u>. If her intuition told her something was wrong, she couldn't be sure what exactly that something was. So Cheryl made a list. It spanned one-and-a-half pages. Unfortunately, it was one-and-a half pages and 12 Days too late.

In true crime time is of the essence, and despite Cheryl's love for her daughter, critical hours, then days then weeks had slipped away and with it traces of Kelsey were slyly and systematically secreted away.

It's because of this lapse of time that ultimately virtually no traces of Kelsey's remains survive or could be recovered, besides a fragment of her tooth and an oily stain in the ground that could also have been an accelerant.

Let's dip back into the trial narrative now and follow Cheryl's entrance into the scene of the crime. She'd contacted Frazee on December 2nd to ask about Kelsey's whereabouts. Frazee minimized things, telling Cheryl he and Kelsey had broken up and Kelsey told him she wanted her own space. Kelsey also wanted her possessions back. Cheryl was surprised by this. Kelsey had never mentioned anything about a break-up, or a breakdown for that matter.

Cheryl asked Frazee to check in on her. Frazee said he had to check on his cows first, but he'd go round to Kelsey's townhome afterwards. This is emblematic in itself. There's almost a biblical analogy in Kelsey's mother asking Frazee to do what he shouldn't have been asked to do in the first place. Breakup or not, a reasonable man in the same circumstances would want to know the mother of his child was safe. And his response to the escalating dilemma?

I need to check on my cows first…

This is an incredible insight into Frazee's authentic psychology, and also his criminal psychology. What kind of guy is Frazee behind the mask, behind the Mr. Nice Guy image?

I need to check on my cows first…

He's a guy worried about his cows. He's a man preoccupied with his livestock, not someone's *actual* life [whether Kelsey's or Kaylee's, or Cheryl's concerns for her daughter]. He's a man anxious about his livestock. He's a man selfishly trying to look after his *live stock*. His *life stock.* He's engrossed in issues of money, cattle prices and fiscal survival. He attaches his own survival, just as Watts did, to his financial health, and wealth. He does this not only as a practical matter, but because this is how a capitalist-consumer society works. It doesn't work if you don't have any money. And so, all other issues are secondary. Everyone else is second to his effort to secure whatever benefits he needs, whatever *life stock* he requires for himself.

Even so, Frazee tells Cheryl he'll go and check up on Kelsey but she won't want to see him. This too is a neat little mirror into his own psychology. He doesn't want to be asked to see her because he doesn't want to see her. He knows where she is. He doesn't want to have to go there even in some fictional explanation because he knows how little is left of her. There *is no explanation* he can give that's not going to put him in an awkward position, and he doesn't want to jeopardize his *life stock.* So he lies.

> *I'll check on her…after I check on my cows.*
> *I must make sure all my cows came home first.*

In the end it's Clint, Kelsey's older brother who convinces Cheryl to contact the cops. Just as in the Watts case, but instead of less than twelve hours after the fact, this was closer to two weeks, the cops respond to a welfare check. The Woodland Park police don't find a chaperone or neighbor on the scene as the Frederick cops did with Nickole Atkinson and Nathaniel Trinastich. They arrive, look in, don't see anything amiss and leave. And the clock ticks on.

When there was still no word on Kelsey, and not much action from the cops,[17] Cheryl promptly boarded a plane with son Clint, and

---

17 The Colorado Bureau of Investigation were eventually contacted on December 4th, on the day after the Berreth's arrival in Woodland Park, and fol-

flew from Idaho to Colorado to find Kelsey. Did Frazee meet Kelsey's mother and older brother [by two years] at the airport? Probably not. He had other fish to fry, or rather, cows to herd…

I need to check on my cows first…

On the way to her townhome from the airport, Cheryl called Frazee to ask if he'd gone looking for Kelsey. This was the last straw. He said he hadn't.

I need to check on my cows first…

That was the last time Cheryl had contact with Frazee. From this point on they were on their own.

#2 CLINT

Cheryl and Clint arrive at Kelsey's townhome late on December 3rd. In the darkness the pair aren't able to make out anything [one assumes they don't enter, and are standing on the outside looking in], so they leave. By now 11 days have passed; what's one more? Perhaps it's better to just sit tight, to wait and see. Maybe Kelsey will turn up the next morning?

But on December 4th when Clint and Cheryl return to Kelsey's townhome it's empty. No sign of her. Frazee – asshole – is still incommunicado, and no help. Cheryl hands Clint the key[18] to the condo. He inserts it.

CLICK.

And let's himself in. As soon as they enter the apartment it seems weird. For starters it's muggy inside. It's too warm. The thermostat has

---

lowing a twelve hour discussion at the Woodland park Police Station.

18 Frazee also had his own key to Kelsey's townhome.

been set to 72 degrees. Kelsey's in the habit of turning it down when leaving her condo. **The garbage doesn't seem right either. It hasn't been taken out.** *There's a strange incongruous whiff in the air. It's difficult to say what it is exactly. Perhaps the smell of the garbage spoiling in the heat, combining with the sweet tint of bleach. Whatever it is there's a strange interplay of fragrances, sweet and a faintly sour odor depending on where they stood in the house.*[19]

Uncovered cinnamon rolls on the stove have turned hard over time. When Clint ventures upstairs, and into Kelsey's bathroom, he finds his younger sister's toothbrush, hair brush and makeup. Her car keys are gone. Her luggage is where it's supposed to be – in the loft.

They spend the night in Kelsey's townhome. The moon and stars wheel overhead, morning comes – December 5th – and Kelsey's absence continues. On Day 13 of Kelsey's disappearance they head to Woodland Park Police Department and don't leave the premises for twelve hours. The police take down <u>a description</u>:[20]

-White female.

-5 feet three inches tall.

-Weight: 110 pounds.

-Brown hair, green eyes.

---

19 <u>Woodland Police sergeant Andrew Leibbrand testified</u> that the air was "thick" inside the Kelsey's townhome from the odor of <u>a scented candle on a warmer.</u> He describes this odor as "pleasant." The warmer was plugged in and on when the police arrived at the scene.

20 The description of Kelsey is later supplemented with <u>CCTV footage from a Safeway in Woodland Park.</u> <u>Kelsey was last seen in this footage</u> wearing a white shirt, tan jacket, blue slacks, a brown purse and white sneakers.

There's nothing much to go on. There's no smoking gun. The length of time is a concern, but <u>in the context of the break-up with a boyfriend it's not setting off any red flags for the cops</u>. The cops reckon: give Kelsey some space. She'll be back.

On December 6th, two long weeks after Kelsey's murder, Clint stoops down in Kelsey's bathroom and notices <u>blood under the bowl of the toilet</u>.

In court, almost a year later <u>Clint would tell a jury</u> hearing evidence on his younger sister's murder: "I went out [of the bathroom] and told my mom 'I think there's blood on the toilet.'"

After this discovery, <u>everything changes</u>.

~

Jackson's Surveillance Camera

The [blood smear] on the outside of the toilet was hidden
from view in a spot where the porcelain is curved, he said.
— <u>The Gazette</u>, referring to Clint Berreth's testimony on
Trial Day 2

When asked how – and why – the police didn't discover any blood when they were summoned to the crime scene, the answer was simple. They weren't looking for blood, they were looking for Kelsey. They were in the mind-set of plain sight, not trying to find what was out of sight.[21]

The discovery of the blood stain doesn't just happen. It's not noticed immediately, along with everything else, and that's a clue in itself. What

---

21 Cognitive bias at the beginning of an investigation – one that is framed as a "disappearance" rather than a homicide – often contaminates the rest of the investigation, and in some cases ultimately undermines the outcome. This occurred in the JonBenét Ramsey case, Madeleine McCann as well as the Amanda Knox case. In all three cases the crime scenes were misrepresented [also known as *staging*] in some way, which led to the cases initially being investigated along bogus lines of inquiry.

   a)   JonBenét Ramsey –kidnapping.

   b)   Madeleine McCann – intruder abduction.

   c)   Amanda Knox – burglary.

they notice they notice *cumulatively*, as Day 12 becomes Day 13, and 13 becomes 14. The killer and the cleaner may have covered their tracks, but one thing they never figured on was Kelsey's family *actually living* in the sanitized crime scene. Who knows, had they not occupied the crime scene, would the blood stain ever have been found? If they had not occupied the crime scene, would Frazee have returned to it one final time and gotten rid of the last remaining clues?

While the pair occupy the townhome, living in it, learning about it – while also contaminating it – and while Kelsey stays missing, they start to notice additional details. The garbage containers aren't in their usual spot. Kelsey's laundry hasn't been done. Her work uniform is on the floor. A broom is laid across Kelsey's bed. Something strange is going on. This isn't like Kelsey at all.

Film from cleaning supplies are in a few places in the townhome. It's streaked over the television, for example. When Cheryl strides by a framed photo of Kelsey with Frazee, she turns it face-down.

All he cares about is his cows...

Cheryl bends down to where Clint is pointing. Then she gets down on her hands and knees on the bathroom floor. She peers closer. An ominous feeling comes over her, silently, like a cloud passing across the white hot face of the sun. Cheryl feels her heart darkening with emotion. With dread. The cloud across the face of the sun is brewing rapidly into a storm with no end to itself. She fumbles for her phone. She snaps an image of the transfer stain and with trembling hands, texts it to CBI agent Slater.

It's at this point that a deadly urgency finally seeps into the investigation. It's not an immediate urgency, but one that seeps, pools and coagulates, the way blood drips out of a broken victim's body. The urgency increases, it expands. Cheryl and Clint are asked to leave the townhome, a sure indicator not only that there is a crime scene, but that Kelsey has been a victim of a crime. Like the storm front roiling in the sky, the scale or scope of the crime is at this point entirely unknown.

The cops enter the scene and exit it. One asks Cheryl and Clint if they've used any cleaning supplies during their two-day sojourn in Kelsey's townhome. Only dish soap to clean dishes. They didn't clean any surfaces, they say.

1 Day: 12 Witnesses

After concluding his testimony, Clint is dismissed. Wisely, the defense don't cross-examine him. Better to leave Clint's radioactive testimony alone. Curiously, Kelsey's neighbor Leslie Jackson isn't the third witness called by the prosecution on Trial Day 3. Instead another neighbor is called – Angela Gerber[22] – an elderly woman who wasn't even in Woodland Park over Thanksgiving.

Thinking about it logically, the prosecution have just sketched out the crime scene and how it was discovered. Why not follow this with the damning evidence from Jackson's video surveillance placing Frazee at the scene? Well, there's a logical reason for that too. It's the fact that the surveillance footage *isn't* damning. Like the surveillance footage in the Watts case, it's too fuzzy to really count as evidence. So what the prosecution need to do is build the rest of the narrative in the minds of the jury. They need to put a mosaic together that starts to form an impression before they see these fuzzy images. And then, sufficiently primed, the jury will fill in the fuzziness with their own imaginations. It's smart trial strategy.

---

22 Angela Gerber was the 3rd prosecution witness.

After Gerber's testimony Kelsey's boss at Doss Aviation – Raymond Siebring[23] – takes the stand. After Siebring, Viehman hands over the prosecutorial baton to her colleague <u>Beth Reed</u>. <u>Reed is shorter than Viehman</u>, with frizzy auburn hair and bookish rectangular rimmed spectacles. Reed calls Woodland Park Police Department Corporal Dena Currin[24] to the stand. It was Currin who took the initial call for the welfare check from Cheryl Berreth on December 2nd. Currin noticed a package by the door, but nothing else out of place. Currin called Kelsey's number, got no answer, and then called Frazee. She recorded her 15-minute conversation with Frazee on her body camera. Frazee told Currin Kelsey wanted space, and also that she'd been to rehab before for alcohol abuse and depression. Frazee also told Currin he'd heard from Kelsey after Thanksgiving, on Sunday November 24th. We will deal with the phone narrative later in this section, in the *Life After Death* chapter.

Currin noted his lack of concern for Kelsey during the call. After her call to Frazee, Currin tried Kelsey again, then called Doss Aviation. There she found out Kelsey had sent them a text saying she'd be out for the week because she was going to see her grandmother. Probably, Frazee had suggested Currin try her employer, knowing full well what they would say. After all this, Currin and a colleague headed to Kelsey's condo [at 15:45], found nothing, called Cheryl back and said they were still investigating, but had found no leads.

After Currin, and a break for lunch, another cop – Woodland Park Police Sergeant Andrew Leibbrand[25] was called to the stand. Leibbrand used a lock bypass tool to gain access to Kelsey's condo. He

---

23 Raymond Siebring was the 4th prosecution witness.

24 Dena Currin was the 5th prosecution witness.

25 Andrew Leibbrand was the 6th prosecution witness.

was one of the first to access the scene. Then it was Woodland Park Police Detective Michael McDaniel's turn.[26] The District Attorney Dan May asked McDaniel about several crime scene photos, among them images depicting Kelsey's two vehicles that hadn't moved in weeks. McDaniel mentioned visits to Kelsey's condo on December 3rd, 4th and 6th. And a cadaver dog alerting on the bumper of Kelsey's car.

After McDaniel prosecutors called Patricia Key,[27] a credit union manager. Key provided fascinating testimony about Frazee approaching her on December 5th, the day before the blood stain was discovered, and two days into the Berreth's occupation of the crime scene. Frazee wanted to know if there was any surveillance footage from the bank's ATM. Frazee told her he was trying to put together a timeline. So Key handed him a photo of his vehicle taken from the ATM's on-board surveillance camera. When Frazee skedaddled, Key immediately contacted the cops. She found his lack of concern weird, Key said in court.

Prior to the recess at 15:00, Teller County Sheriff's Deputy Chris Paulsen[28] took the stand. Paulsen met Frazee at a restaurant in Colorado Springs on December 4th, the day after the Berreths arrived in Woodland Park to investigate. Paulsen asked Frazee for his phone.

After the recess, an employee from a Woodland Park Verizon store – David Felis[29] – took the stand. Many of Felis' statements corresponded to Patricia Key's. Felis said he saw Frazee when he visited the store on December 11th. Felis and Key's respective testimonies are

---

26 Michael McDaniel was the 7th prosecution witness.

27 Patricia Key was the 8th prosecution witness.

28 Chris Paulsen was the 9th prosecution witness.

29 David Felis was the 10th prosecution witness.

tremendously significant, along with the dates when they saw Frazee. We'll be interrogating Felis and Key in the *INTERTEXUALITIES* section in more detail.

Penultimately, on Trial Day 2, after calling around a dozen witnesses, the District Attorney finally called Leslie Jackson.[30]

#3 JACKSON

Leslie Jackson's <u>wooden fence</u>, painted a dark chocolate brown, is <u>adjacent to Kelsey's property</u> #269. Fortuitously for this case, Jackson had not one but three cameras, including one directed at her bedroom window while taking in the boundary fence and Kelsey's front door in its peripheral vision. The Arlo system is both sound and motion activated.

At 12:36:52 Jackson's <u>Arlo</u> security system[31] <u>auto-emailed Jackson an alert</u>. It was Frazee arriving at #269 while Kelsey was out. Did Frazee know Jackson's camera was trained on the entrance? Probably – like Chris Watts – he did know. But Frazee likely reasoned Thanksgiving was the ideal time for the surveillance footage to expire, and be recorded over, and he was right – it was. What he didn't know was that there might be some back-up default system activated, screengrabbing a snapshot whenever there was an alert and auto-emailing Jackson in real time.

Whether Frazee was aware of this or not, he – like Watts – took precautions not to be caught on camera *in flagrante delicto*, or more *in flagrante* than he ultimately was. Just as Watts is never actually seen moving bodies over his driveway, we don't see Frazee carrying a murder

---

30 Leslie Jackson was the 11th prosecution witness.

31 The Arlo surveillance system can be regarded as a counterpart to Vivint, the digital security system used by the Watts family.

weapon, nor do we see him in blood splattered clothing. This raises the question, how did Frazee get the wooden baseball bat into the Kelsey's condo? And in the same way, how did he remove Kelsey's body without being seen by that Arlo camera?

During the trial it was said that Frazee arrived at Kelsey's condo early, then left to run some errands. The impression is that he made a mistake. That he arrived early, too early, then left and came back later. What's more likely is that on Frazee's first trip, alone, entering at 12:36:52, he brought the baseball bat with him, carried under a sweater.

One can clearly <u>see something in his left hand as he unlocks the door</u>. Bear in mind, if Frazee knows about the camera peering down at him from its perch on the neighboring property, he also knows the fence framing the alley is relatively high, almost hip high. So any object carried low enough could be concealed, theoretically, just as the tree foliage and side of Watts' truck concealed him – largely – from view.

One has to say, if both killers knew they were being captured by surveillance [and it appears they did know], it was not only extremely brazen to carry out the crime under the guise of the camera regardless, but an incredible gambit. One slip and the game was potentially up.

If the Jackson footage is pretty damning, and it is, what was also pretty damning was the fact that Jackson never contacted the cops about it. She knew about the footage, had looked at it, but even though she saw Frazee in the screengrabs, didn't see anything suspicious about it [unlike the neighbor in the Watts case].

This impression of Frazee not appearing to be doing anything out of the ordinary shows to what extent he was able to pull the wool over eyes, even when the brains behind them knew Kelsey was gone, and footage showed him coming and going. In a sense. Jackson was one of the strongest prosecution witnesses, but also one of the weakest, just as Krystal Kenney was.

Landscape and Memory/Memory and Landscape

"I bought some sweet potatoes[32] in case you wanted sweet potato casserole but I forgot to get pecans you should get if you want some."— Kelsey Berreth's final legitimate text to Frazee, sent at 12:41 shortly after leaving a Safeway store. Frazee didn't reply to it.

Leslie Jackson noticed something odd on November 22nd, when she was away from home, at her mother's house for Thanksgiving. Her phone kept buzzing on the table. Six or seven times more than usual it went BBZZZZZZT. Eventually Jackson put the phone somewhere else [while Kelsey was being bludgeoned to death] so it wouldn't disturb the rest of her Thanksgiving.

---

32 One of Shan'ann Watts' final messages texted to Chris Watts, was sent at 21:09 on August 12th, 2018, a few short before her death. It read: "What kind of vegetables do you want with dinner tomorrow?" Watts answered curtly: "Green beans." Shan'ann told she would buy them "tomorrow from Costco as well as other food items.

The final witness called on Trial Day 4 was Chad Mininger,[33] a digital expert tasked with extracting the data from Jackson's phone[34] and other devices, as well as compiling and interpreting the digital narrative.

Mininger sketched a slightly different digital scene to the one Jackson provided for the jury. Using a PowerPoint presentation in the court room, Mininger used Google Earth to illustrate the layout of Kelsey's home vis-à-vis Jackson's [on the left, to the west] and Gerber's –sharing a drywall on the right, to the east]. What Mininger was doing was providing a context to the scene. Then he did the same in terms of the digital ecosystem.

He provided a precedent in terms of the alerts on November 21st. Jackson's bedroom, Mininger noted, sent just four alerts. On the 22nd there were 27 alerts. The majority of these occurred around noon, around noon and 13:20 and then a final blitz between 16:20 and 16:30. **Frazee appeared in 11 of these 27 alerts.** On the 23rd Jackson's bedroom camera alerted three times, and on the 24th, three times again.

Mininger showed images of Kelsey entering her home at 03:54 on November 22nd with a baby carrier. Another image showed Kelsey at her door at 11:56, presumably leaving to do grocery shopping at Safeway with her daughter. Exactly 40 minutes later, at 12:36 the bedroom camera showed Frazee at the condo for the first time that day. He arrived alone, entered, then – at 12:37:22 – left again.[35]

---

33 Chad Mininger was the prosecution's 12th witness.

34 Mininger used Cellebrite technology for the extraction, the same system used to extract data off Watts' phone, Shan'ann's phone and Kessinger's phone.

35 When Frazee was captured leaving, it didn't appear he was carrying anything, whereas when he arrived, it was clear that he was carrying something under his left arm.

Court adjourned on Day 3 with these images burned into the jurors' minds.

Landscape

At a vertiginous 14 115 feet [4 302 meters] Pike's Peak is the highest summit of the southern Front Range of the Rocky Mountains. No mountain east of its position is higher. It's a 21 mile hike from Woodland Park to Pike's Peak and 31 miles from the Frazee ranch, near Florissant.

Early Spanish explorers referred to the granite extrusion as El Capitán, *The Leader*. From hundreds of miles around, this peak dominates the landscape, and with it, its history and memories remain in the minds of those who live in the area. Its silhouette etches into each day, and as the grains of night thicken, the peak is there – always there.

Conditions at the summit are like the conditions of another planet. Pike's Peak has a polar climate. On an average afternoon, winds gust up to 100 miles per hour. The mountain has towered over various dramas, over the millennia, some manmade, some shaping the fates of man, some shifting the fate of landscapes and memories. One of them, occurring within the conflagration of men and minerals that was named after the mountain itself [the Pike's Peak Gold Rush] was the Mount Pisgah Hoax in the spring of 1884. Gold ore was added to barren ore in a fraud[36] calculated to *inspire* a gold rush [which it did], thus inflating property values [which it did].

According to the *Denver Post*:

---

36 The *Denver Post* highlights other similar scams in Colorado to the Mount Pisgah Hoax. These include Garfield's "Cave of Gold" and several others.

Enterprising Cañon merchants paid two prospectors to dig a hole 18 feet deep, salt it with gold from South Park, then return to Cañon for an assay of their dirt — $2,000 of gold to the ton. Word got out, and soon special trains to Cañon were packed, the wagon roads to McIntyre were jammed and Cañon merchants enjoyed record sales of picks, pans and pinto beans.

Not surprisingly, the boom collapsed. When real gold was discovered in Cripple Creek a decade later, prospectors were circumspect. While some were leery, in reality the pots of gold of Cripple Creek constituted Colorado's last gold rush. The Independence lode, located between breccia deposits, became the Independence mine, one of the largest gold strikes in America. When capitalist W.S. Stratton got involved in the site, he rapidly rose to become Cripple Creek's first millionaire. The fool's gold and fake gold rush – the hoax in '84 – ultimately gave way to the most productive gold-producing district in Colorado, and the third-most productive in America.

The terrain was difficult and treacherous to work. A five-mile tunnel was dug in 1907 below Cripple Creek to drain the mines. Today, only one Colorado mine continues with gold production – the Cripple Creek & Victor[37] Gold Mine.

But the shadow of the great mountain has loomed over other conundrums, besides the glitter of fool's gold, and real gold. In 1896 two fire disasters swept through Cripple Creek. The first occurred in April, burning half the town to ash. Four days later most of what was left went up in smoke too. As a result, most of the buildings in modern day Cripple Creek date from the year after the fire swept through the town and razed it to the ground.

---

37 Victor, another mining community, is the sister city to Cripple Creek.

If the fortunes of Cripple Creek were destroyed by fire, and squandered by fraud and fakery, they were also forged in fire. The gold-bearing area was once the core of an ancient volcano, way back during the Oligocene era. 30 million years ago an area spanning 8 500 square miles produced around a dozen volcanoes.

Cripple Creek

What's in a name? Cripple Creek got its name from the frequency of livestock crossing the creek and injuring themselves. The Roosevelt Tunnel caused the stream to drain into it [and out of the mines], thereby lowering the water table by 1 500 feet throughout the Cripple Creek mining district. Good for gold mining. Bad for ranching.

Memory

Does the geological history, the shape and silhouette of the landscape, and of mountains, have any influence on the conscious or subconscious mind? The ancient injuries to animals, the fires raging through towns, the ebb and flow of gold and flocks, some defrauded, others enriched – did any of these stories make a play on the story forming in Frazee's mind? Because make no mistake, a crime must first happen in a murderer's mind before it can happen in the real world. The story must first form in his heart before it touches anyone else.

We know that Frazee salted the memory of the community with fake stories of Kelsey – that she was a bad mother, that she was an alcoholic, that she wanted him to have the baby because she couldn't look after her, and didn't want to. Where did Frazee get this idea of salting?

Because of her job Kelsey was often elsewhere. Sometimes she was flying. Sometimes she was on ground. But most of the time it was safe to say she was far from Cripple Creek. The people knew Frazee, they didn't really know her, and *vice versa*.

As a rancher Frazee spent long hours walking the woods, getting his boots dirty, surveying the landscape. When you walk the terrain *you feel it*. The locals share in the stories. They ruminate. They dream. And in such a situation the landscape and memory can become a canvas on which to commit a crime. He could destroy her reputation because she was always away. And so, once she disappeared she wouldn't be missed. He could see to that.

Unfortunately for Frazee, it wasn't only the great mountain that had handy memories of mischief, lingering in the minds of men. Digital eyes and ears were everywhere, and even if you thought you knew where all of them were, there was always the one that you didn't think about…

Poking Holes and Not His Brother's Keeper

"A camera at Williams Log Home Furniture spotted Patrick Frazee at 16:36 driving with the black box in the bed of the pickup reoriented from how it was four hours earlier." — <u>Lance Benzel</u>, The Gazette

November 5th, a Tuesday, and Trial day 3 in the Patrick Frazee criminal murder trial, dawned bright blue and crispy cold in Cripple Creek. Frazee arrived in green-striped prison garb, then changed into a red checkered dress shirt and khakis.

Tuesday, for both counsels, was all about reconstructing and deconstructing a timeline. The prosecutors would set up the timeline, then the defense would cross-examine and try to poke holes in it. The real insight, the one no seemed to notice or care about, was the finances. But Frazee did care. He cared that his own brother Sean was going to expose him in ways only a brother's keeper – now estranged[38] – possibly can.

---

38 When asked about his relationship with Frazee, <u>Sean said</u>:
"I don't know that we've been on bad terms, we just haven't been close."

Before we get to the elder Frazee brother's testimony on the murderous defendant – Patrick – let's review a handful of the other witnesses. The day started with Chad Mininger resuming his testimony from the previous day. Mininger pointed out that <u>Jackson's surveillance was just 16 feet from Berreth's front door</u>. Although it had an unobstructed view of the top portion of the entrance to Kelsey's townhome, <u>the bottom area was obstructed</u> by the neighboring perimeter fence. One of the defenses arguments was that <u>this barrier prevented one from seeing anything being carried into or for that matter</u>, out of, the condo.

The high point for the defense was when Steigerwald questioned the lighting of two almost simultaneous images, but showing very different lighting conditions. According to *The Gazette*, Steigerwald chided Mininger:

"I know you're a forensic cell phone reconstruction expert, but that's not the way the sun moves, is it?"

Mininger dodged this allegation, saying it may have been a cloudy day, and most of the screengrabs from midday and going into the afternoon do indicate a sunless scenario for the most part. Interestingly, in the discovery released to the public, there are no images with shadows, and none that can be juxtaposed where the lighting suddenly appears different.

In any event, the attack forced Mininger to acknowledge that his analysis assumed the captured images examined on Jackson's phone were in chronological order – when they may not have been.

According to *The Gazette:*

If [Jackson] happened to click on those cell phone alerts out of sequence, Mininger conceded that his reconstructed timeline would be flawed. Timing is a key issue [because] Frazee...previously told police he stopped by Berreth's condo only once on Thanksgiving Day to get their baby, and that he left at noon.

There were other issues too, for the prosecution to get through, most notably <u>the black tote</u>. The difficult question facing the prosecution was that even if they placed Frazee at the scene, there was no footage showing him removing Kelsey from the scene. In fact there is <u>no black tote visible anywhere</u>, coming or going. So how was Kelsey removed from the scene? We'll deal with this question in the final chapters, but first let's find out why the tote is relevant to begin with.

The first point to address is that regardless of whether a tote was used to transport Kelsey, and regardless of whether there's any footage of Frazee moving from the front door, Kelsey was seen entering the apartment and was never seen again. We have a similar scenario with Shan'ann Watts in the Chris Watts case. She's seen entering her home at 01:48 but we never see her alive after that. In the same way as the Frazee case, Watts is also seen making several trips into and out of his home very early in the morning. We don't see any bodies, but we do see the perpetrator moving from an exit point to his vehicle and back on numerous occasions. Sometimes what we see is obscured, but what is clear is something is going on at a critical time, and the movements are atypical. It's atypical for Watts to have his truck backed up, and it's atypical to have all this loading and unloading going on for close to half an hour. In the Frazee case it occurs over the course of around three hours.[39]

---

39 The surveillance camera screengrabs do not distinguish between Frazee entering the townhome and leaving. Unlike the Watts video, the surveillance screengrabs are stills with no motion attached to them. This added further uncertainty to what the surrounding movements actually were, before and

After Mininger, the prosecution called three witnesses in rapid succession. Huber and Currin were from local law enforcement, while Stephanie Courtney was a District Attorney investigator.

In its coverage of Trial Day 3, _The Gazette_ described a camera at Williams Log Home Furniture in Woodland Park capturing Frazee driving away from Kelsey's condo at <u>12:44:33</u> and <u>again</u> at <u>16:40</u>. The actual times for these captures are minus approximately six minutes, based on the analysis of Jason Memmer, a sales and delivery employee at Williams Furniture in Woodland Park. Memmer, who testified after Sean Frazee, was also in charge of the store's cameras. We will deal with Memmer at the start of the next chapter _My Mistress' Eyes_.

According to _The Gazette_ when Frazee's red pickup was spotted the second time:

...a black box in the bed of his pickup **was reoriented** from how it had been four hours earlier. Prosecutors presented it as evidence that Frazee had Berreth's body in the hard plastic case...The defense suggested that Frazee had manipulated the box when he was putting away supplies he'd purchased at Walmart, including a large bag of dog food.

It's not clear exactly what the prosecutors are driving at. <u>In the 16:40 image</u> [time based on the surveillance clock] one can clearly see the two silvery-white metal clasps of the black tote box facing the viewer. In <u>the 12:44 image</u> the two silver-white clasps aren't visible. In an <u>image taken from a Conoco gas station</u> two days later at 16:35 on November 24th, the black tote that was in the rear of the pickup is no longer there.

Another aspect to note is shortly after we see the last known picture of Kelsey with Kaylee and Frazee [at <u>13:23:48</u>] we see Frazee again, this time alone, <u>at 13:24:16</u>. In this second image shown by the District

---

after the stills were captured.

Attorney Dan May during trial, he pointed out that Frazee appears to be holding something in his right hand as he closes [or opens] the door. Three hours later Frazee is captured again, again with his back to the surveillance camera, <u>at 16:20:59</u>. In this image Frazee is holding Kaylee in one arm, and over his right shoulder one can barely make out the opposite wall [which <u>Kenney would later testify was covered in a wide arc of blood spatter</u>].

There are additional captures of Frazee without Kaylee at <u>16:24:35</u>, carrying Kaylee at <u>16:26:49</u>, carrying Kaylee at <u>16:27:14</u>, carrying Kaylee at <u>16:28:34</u>, and without Kaylee at <u>16:29:17</u> and <u>16:30:31</u>.

But Steigerwald's point was hard to ignore:

None of the pictures show Frazee carrying a large black tote…

Irrespective of the movements of the black tote after Frazee left Kelsey's townhome that fateful day, the defense had a point in questioning how it got into the bed of the pickup, and whether it had *anything* to do with Kelsey, or Kelsey's murder. If it did, frustratingly there was simply no direct evidence showing that. Mininger's explanation for this seemingly inexplicable void in the state's case was that "<u>there's a void between Frazee and the door.</u>" Mininger admitted he couldn't tell exactly what it – "the void" – was.[40]

True Crime Rocket Science observes *no void* between Frazee and the door. The screengrabs seem to prove a black tote wasn't used

---

40 According to <u>*The Denver Channel*</u> reporting on Trial Day 3, Mininger tried to account for the "void" between Frazee and the door [imputing a black tote one imagines].

[Mininger said he] can't tell exactly what it [the void] is…[and] some cameras may have distorted lenses, which could alter the perception of the void. [Mininger] said [although] the cameras are of good quality…zooming in makes the image pixelated.

through the front door, rather than that it was. In addition, and this is a clue to what follows, the screengrabs show that particular front door exit was likely not used to remove/move Kelsey's body.

4 SEAN

When Frazee's older brother Sean took the stand, the reporters in court noted how Frazee seemed to be become more attentive. The older brother spoke quietly, and didn't appear to make eye contact with his sibling while on the witness stand. In contrast, Frazee eyeballed his sibling,[41] taking notes as his brother spoke softly about the Frazee family, and Frazee in particular.

If the defense had succeeded in landing a few blows of reasonable doubt in terms of the credibility of the surveillance footage [and they had], as well as the admissibility of the prosecution's Tote Theory, [ditto], Sean's testimony tended to bolster both. More one than the other, perhaps, but Sean's testimony brought another dimension of color to that hazy Thanksgiving Day. If the screengrabs provided silent witness, Sean's testimony broke that silence and suddenly made things feel louder and yes, clearer.

Sean said he drove to Florissant with his family to spend the Thanksgiving holiday with his mother and brother. His mother was around, Patrick – for most of the day – was not. Frazee finally arrived at 17:00, and then managed to miss a 90-minute dinner as well. Crucially, Sean's testimony corresponded with the timeline of the surveillance screengrabs and CCTV video. It was also clear from basic logistics that if Frazee was captured at 16:30 in Woodland Park, and arrived home at the ranch near Florissant at 17:00, then he likely drove straight home

---

41 In the words of *The Denver Channel*, Frazee appeared to look at [Sean] with more interest than with other witnesses.

from Kelsey's townhome – a drive that is typically in the order of 20-30 minutes.

But the most gripping aspect of Sean's testimony was his first-hand account of seeing his brother walk in after spending hours doing the devil's work inside Kelsey's nondescript townhome. According to *The Gazette*, Sean – speaking in a monotone with little emotion – recalled "a nice evening" to the jury.

On Thanksgiving Day 2018, Sean arrived at the ranch with his wife and children around 14:30.[42] *Only his mother was there, he said. They had dinner shortly afterward for about 60 to 90 minutes and Patrick still hadn't showed up.*

Frazee called home – the landline – at 16:30, to say he was on his way. This also matches the Jackson surveillance footage. The last screengrab is from 16:30:31. This suggests the moment Frazee was done cleaning and loading Kelsey's body, he called home. But there's something strange about the timestamps and the way the story unfolds, doesn't it? It all seems to be stock-standard times. Kelsey is home at about 13:30. Frazee's brother arrives at the ranch at 14:30. Frazee calls home at 16:30. Frazee arrives home at 17:00. Sean and his family depart

---

42 Frazee must have known his brother was attending Thanksgiving. The crime was committed at around 13:30, so one imagines Frazee anticipated being done with the clean-up by 14:00 so he could get back home and show his face by 14:30. It's possible Frazee totally underestimated the length of time he needed to commit the crime, move the body and clean up the worst evidence. On the other hand, he may have counted on his mother and brother vouching for him – giving him an alibi – if there were ever any questions. This moment right here, with Frazee's brother testifying against him, demonstrates that Frazee made a critical miscalculation in this regard.

at 19:30. It feels as if the premeditation was part of a timed schedule, doesn't it?

There's also this:

Only his mother was there, he said. They had dinner shortly afterward…

Why is it that the whole family didn't simply wait for Frazee and Kaylee to arrive home? Why have dinner shortly after 14:30? Why not have dinner together when everyone was together, after 17:00?

In addition, there's no mention from Sean about Kelsey's absence. It's implied here that Sheila Frazee didn't expect Kelsey to join them, nor for that matter did she expect Patrick or Kaylee. Why not? If she did expect them surely they would have called him and waited for him to join them. After all, when are meals more family oriented than on Thanksgiving?

According to <u>*The Gazette*</u>:

When he did arrive, [Patrick] brought Kaylee in. "And we played with her…" Then **Patrick made some food for himself and Kaylee.** *Patrick spent about half the time [after he arrived] outside doing chores.*[43] *After dessert, Sean and his family left at about 19:30.*

Now it may be that the middle son didn't want to be part of a meal if his brother was present, and everyone understood this. If that's true, it does seem as if the whole family was present when dessert was served. Did anyone ask where Kelsey was or where Frazee had been the whole afternoon? Evidently not. If not, why not?

---

43 One of these chores was – supposedly – feeding the horses.

When the prosecutor asked Sean whether his brother was on the phone throughout his visit, Sean couldn't say. When asked whether he noticed a black tote in the back of Frazee's truck, Sean said he didn't notice. Some reports indicate that Frazee had parked the truck out of sight, while others suggest Frazee simply said he'd parked it out of sight. Sean added that it wouldn't be unusual for there to be a black box in the back of his truck. None of this testimony feels particularly convincing, does it?

Prosecutor Dan May also asked the elder Frazee brother about the Frazee family ranch. Sean said his mother had lived at the ranch for 20 years, and so had his brother. Sean admitted he hadn't been close to his brother for the past two to three years.[44] 20 years for a 33-year-old man is basically his entire life.

When this issue came up, a dozen pieces of the Frazee puzzle suddenly slotted into place. Can you see why? The fact that Frazee was a handsome, sturdy rancher was always significant, but the insight that he'd been living on the ranch *with his mother* meant that dynamic was of prime importance. It clearly indicated Frazee wasn't the independent bachelor he appeared to be, he was in fact still a *dependent*, in terms of his mother.

This aspect also clearly differentiated him from his two siblings, sister Erin and brother Sean, neither of whom seemed to like their middle sibling very much. Was it because their mother favored him? Or was it because of what "favoring" may have implied, specifically with reference to how an inheritance might be divvied up? Who should be allocated more? Shouldn't the loyal son, tending to his mother, supporting the family business hands-on be given the lion's share in the

---

44 A family grudge match was also part of the family dynamics in the Chris Watts case immediately preceding the murders.

$400 000 that was up for grabs? Or did the siblings who had gone off to seek their fortunes elsewhere deserve more? Now, when the patriarch had died, they returned as prodigals[45] to collect on what was theirs. But what *was* theirs, and who decided on a fair cutting up of the pie?

The biggest moment on Trial Day 3 came from a tiny word Sean added in his response to a question. The prosecutor covered the fact that the father of the Frazee family died on August 28th, 2018. Bearing in mind the trial was heard 14 months after Robert Frazee's death, when Sean said they were *still* going through his estate, he meant the siblings had been squabbling over their inheritance from the beginning. One of the more contentious pieces of the pie: *how to carve property among several beneficiaries.* Bear in mind if Frazee used the ranch as his livelihood with his mother, what would have happened to that livelihood if a significant portion was sliced up and given to the siblings?

When the prosecutor asked Sean when he found out for the first time Kelsey was missing, Sean said December 3rd. December 3rd was basically when the outside world started finding out, beginning with Kelsey's mother, her brother and from there the Woodland Park cops, the CBI, FBI, the media and everyone else. But what about Frazee's inner world? If Frazee was living with his mother, didn't she notice that Kaylee's mother had been gone all week, and the week following?

Sean said his brother told him Kelsey's grandmother was sick, and suggested her going to visit her grandmother without informing anyone was one possibility. This in itself was an interesting ruse. Here Frazee was both using a known quality of Kelsey's [her care and consideration for her grandmother] and perhaps her quiet nature [not telling anyone]

---

45 Prodigal means "reckless spender". Was the prodigal son Frazee all along, regardless of where he lived or whose allegiance he supposedly kept?

to account for her movements. Think about these dynamics from the perspective of Frazee's psychology though. He wants to care for someone – Kaylee. Or does he want *her* grandmother [Sheila, who is infirm] to care for her? He is the one not telling anyone where Kelsey is, not Kelsey.

Frazee also told his brother Kelsey and him were separated, that she was having an affair, had "alcohol issues" and had gone into rehab before. Frazee speculated that she may have gone to find help for her "issues", but once more, not told anyone her plans. This indirectly portrayed her as a reckless, unreliable, philandering mother, a description more apt to Frazee than Kelsey.

Frazee – during the same call – also told his brother he'd gotten a call from Doss Aviation. It was regarding their intention to cancel Kaylee's health insurance because Kelsey hadn't been working enough. There is a lot loaded in this snippet as well. After falling pregnant Kelsey had opted to work fewer hours. By working part time Kaylee's health insurance was in jeopardy. It may be that Frazee figured if he killed Kelsey sooner than later, her employer would take care of the health benefits *while they were still in effect*. There is some indication that the status of Kelsey's insurance in terms of her employer was due for an imminent overhaul, either in December or soon after that.

Sean, a Colorado Spring cop, said his brother's demeanor during the call concerned him at the time [though evidently not enough for him to call the cops]. On December 4th the brothers were face to face in a parking lot when a police officer approached them both. The officer asked Frazee for his phone. Sean countered, asking if they had a warrant. The officer said he didn't, but planned on getting one. Sean told his younger sibling to hand over his phone. Frazee did.

When Sean left the stand, he glanced over at his brother, turned his head, and in a dramatic motion that the reporters present all caught, rolled his eyes. The ongoing family feud wasn't over. It was left to Dan May to instruct the jury on something that was beyond obvious. May told them that *financial pressures* would "factor into" the prosecution's case,[46] whatever that meant.

------

46 Curiously, the District Attorney in the Watts case tended to be more dismissive of the financial pressures. During the sentencing hearing he equated the financial pressures of the Watts family with those of ordinary Americans, thus making the financial disaster gyrating over #2825 Saratoga Trail seem normal, when it was anything but. The same deteriorating financial maelstrom appeared to have mired Frazee in murderous thoughts of blood and gold.

Special Agent Charles DeFrance, Slater and The Missing Link

"It is a mistake to look too far ahead. Only one link of the chain of destiny can be handled at a time." — Winston Churchill

Between Sean Frazee's testimony and the FBI's Special Agent Charles DeFrance's testimony, two witnesses were called. One was Jason Memmer, from Williams Furniture in Woodland Park. The other was Stephanie Courtney, an investigator with the DA's office, who testified just after 11:30. We will deal with Memmer and Courtney's testimony outside of the trial chronology.

#5 DeFRANCE[47]

DeFrance took the court through the relatively haphazard and mostly fruitless search over a weeklong period starting on December 21st, and ending – mercifully – with a breakthrough on January 21st, one long month after Kelsey had vanished.

The problem with a sanitized crime scene, and an unknown time of death [in this case, the status of the deceased herself was unknown

---

47 FBI Special Agent Charles DeFrance was the 17th witness called by the prosecution.

at the time] is where to begin? Where do you start looking? DeFrance searched the Frazee ranch on December 14th and 15th, as well as the house on the property. They didn't find much. They didn't really have any leads three weeks into Kelsey's disappearance. Things weren't looking good at all.

DeFrance described in court how his team of investigators spent two full days processing Frazee's red truck. What did they find? Zip. Then it was back to Kelsey's home, then back to the ranch. Frazee had gotten law enforcement to chase their own tails, and each tick of the clock meant the case was getting colder and colder.

The prosecutor – Dan May – asked the FBI agent what evidence was collected from Frazee's home on December 15th. "Banking documents," DeFrance answered. What else was collected? Financial statements, receipts inside an Ent Credit Union folder,[48] and <u>custody documents</u> left on top of the television stand.

With precious little to go on, the cops were going on the only thing they really had on Frazee - *financial pressures*. Other receipts were from Walmart, a receipt from a Waste Management plant, and finally copies Frazee had requested of surveillance photos from the Ent Credit Union ATM. Besides this, the paper trail also included blank checks, banking records as well as two letters inside envelopes from Farm Credit addressed to Frazee.

The Walmart receipt was dated November 22nd and timestamped 13:50. Frazee seemed to be trying to convince the authorities he was in Walmart when Kelsey vanished. Ominously, DeFrance found five

---

48 Handwritten notes on the inside of an envelope appeared to show Frazee's alibi, or at least the alibi he intended to offer to the authorities when they came for him.

deposits at an ATM on November 22nd, along with a single withdrawal. This set of circumstances, more than most, reinforces the notion that Frazee murdered Kelsey for money.

DeFrance, prompted by the prosecutor, also took the court through the handwritten to-do list on the envelope:

Approximately 12:30, pick up Kaylee.[49]

Meet and exchange from parking area at her house.

Approximately 12:45, Ent bank deposits.

Approximately 1:30, leave Walmart.

Drive 40 miles to check on feed, water cattle.

I need to check on my cows first…

Approximately 2:45, feed, water, check on cattle.

Approximately 3:45, drive home for Thanksgiving dinner.

Approximately 4:30, get home.

Just going by the bogus schedule, notice the standard timestamps: 12:30, 12:45, 1:30, 2:45, 3:45, 4:30. It's likely when Frazee premeditated the murders, he had similar broad timestamps in mind that he wanted to stick to, if at all possible. The fake alibi was powerful evidence not because it provided an alibi, but because the Jackson surveillance footage conclusively proved that it didn't. This alone was strong evidence that Frazee was hiding something. Was it an affair? What more than that?

The state then called another FBI Agent to the stand, Stephanie Benitez. It was Benitez's job to photograph the scene of the crime. Benitez simply confirmed the photos taken of documents on the top of Frazee's television in the lounge *were related to custody issues.*

---

49 Source: *The Denver Channel*

After Benitez Woodland Park Police Commander Chris Adams was called to the stand. Adams was involved in checking Kelsey's browsing history [explored in more detail in the *Life After Death – The Phone Narrative* chapter]. Adams noted the blood found in the bathroom in Kelsey's townhome, but admitted they didn't know who it belonged to, or whether it meant anything. Adams also noted that the investigation "stagnated", but that it regained momentum once they applied for cell phone records.

On December 4th, two days after the police were alerted by Kelsey's mother, Adams contacted the FBI and CBI for assistance. One of the agents that responded to Adams' call for additional resources was CBI Agent Gregg Slater.

#6 SLATER[50]

<u>*The Denver Channel*</u> highlighted Slater's testimony on Trial Day 3 as part of its *10 Key Moments*, published on November 16th, after the first two weeks of testimony had concluded.

Slater admitted to the court that coming into this case with a 10-day handicap from when Kelsey was last seen, was "a big disadvantage."

They had to start somewhere, so they started with Kaylee. Was she safe? The police didn't know. They hadn't followed up. Slater made sure they did. It turned out she was safe. She was with her father.

It was Slater who determined Frazee was paying Kelsey $700 a month in child support. It was Slater who followed up on the custody documents on the top of Frazee's TV. It turned out to be a fee agreement. Frazee was committing to paying his attorney a certain sum in a preliminary process that would culminate in a custody battle for Kaylee. Slater also discovered that the custody paperwork was never

---

50 CBI Agent Gregg Slater was the 20th witness called by the prosecution.

filed in court. No mention is made what the attorney fee was, but it's possible, and even likely, Frazee felt he couldn't stomach the fee and the associated costs. Make sense?

Slater also alerted the court to a certified letter sent by the Farm Credit Bureau. It indicated Frazee had defaulted on a huge $72 000 loan. It had matured on December 1st. Slater said the letter was dated December 5th, 2018. While they were going through Frazee's finances, they intermittently checked Kelsey's. Her accounts were completely dormant. The only activity appeared to be in September 2018.

It's unfortunate there was no coverage inside the court while this particular aspect was covered. It would have been interesting to see Frazee's expression and body language. Would he have appeared nervous, or uncomfortable, while the court discussed his desperate and desperately fraught financial situation circa November/December 2018?

I need to check on my cows first…

According to Slater, the investigation reignited when Kelsey's brother Clint texted him very early in the morning on December 6th. This text contained an image of the blood stain on the base of the toilet, as well as a second trace discovered on the inside of the door knob of the bathroom door.

Slater alerted Commander Adams and Woodland Police Chief De Young. He made an urgent request there and then for a crime scene team to be dispatched to the condo to do a canine search along with chemical testing. Kelsey's mother and brother were asked to leave the premises, and their belongings were seized.[51] Bluestar Forensic Blood

---

51 Cheryl and Clint's belongings were returned to them after 1-2 months.

Reagent was used throughout the scene. When the reagent glowed blue it meant a positive result for blood. It glowed bright blue.

According to *The Denver Channel*:

Once [law enforcement] discovered blood, foul play became a factor in the investigation, and they started looking for Frazee.

As alluded to earlier, the fact that they found blood traces suggested foul play may have occurred, but they were by no means certain. There was some blood, but not much. They weren't even certain if the blood belonged to Kelsey, and if it did, what it meant.

The next step was seizing Frazee's phone. Had Frazee gotten rid of his phone, or done a better job of erasing the history of the device [as Nichol Kessinger had done a few months prior] perhaps the investigation would have stuttered and eventually come to a dead end. Instead, investigators started looking at Frazee's call history.

Significantly, a call to Idaho was made on November 22nd between 16:30 and 16:40.[52] It would take a while for investigators to find out who that Idaho number belonged to.

Trial Day 3 concluded with a juror asking a question. The juror wanted to know if the cadaver dog searching inside Kelsey's condo alerted to anything. Slater said it didn't. Then a follow-up question. When did the cadaver dog go inside the condo? Slater said it went in on December 4th.

---

52 Presumably, having just exited the crime scene, and while he was *en route* to Thanksgiving dessert with his family [with Kelsey's red rag doll body stuffed in the tote in the bed of the truck] that was when Frazee told Krystal Kenney: *You've got a mess to clean up.*

Kenney said she would do it, just not right then.

Trial Day 3 seemed to end prematurely, on a whimper. At 15:13 the jury was excused. Was the prosecution running out of steam? A giant balloon hung like some kind of ghastly, bloated apparition, over the small town of Cripple Creek. It was so big, this inflatable effigy of lies and deception, it felt to some like it was blotting out the sun. Everything good and bright in the world had been lost. The world had turned to sunless shadow, the fields to dry tinder.

On Trial Day 4, the prosecution would lift a needle to that balloon, and when it burst, it would be deafening.

My Mistress' Eyes

"She had very, very good reasoning for whatever it is she may or may not have done." — Michelle Stein, Krystal Kenney's friend

Calling Krystal Kenney was just part of a routine check.

Initially, Frazee's call records were a muddle. How to tell which numbers meant anything from the strings of meaningless names and numbers? Then something unusual happened. As investigators worked to decipher the cell phone data, going backwards through the timeline they noticed <u>Kelsey's phone had pinged near Gooding, Idaho on November 25th</u>. *Three days after she'd disappeared. Three days after she was last seen.*

Eventually, investigators put two and two together. There was an Idaho number on Frazee's phone too. He'd called that number on November 22nd. Law enforcement found the Idaho number on Frazee's phone belonged to Kenney. So they called Kenney to ask her a few questions.

Calling Krystal Kenney was just part of a routine check.

If Kenney had played her cards better, the cops would have simply gone on through the list and questioned others as well. But Kenney didn't play her cards very well. And ultimately, everything unravelled for her, for Frazee and the whole scheme. Now it all came down to this – a day in court where she would blow the lid off the Frazee case. If she played her cards straight, she would get off [for the most part] and his chances of beating the prosecution's case against him would sink like a stone. The question was: would the jury believe her? Would her story [and thus the prosecution's case] hold up?

Trial Day 4, a Wednesday, dawned glassy blue with feathers of cirrus streaking high above the historic court building. The Judge emphasized strict guidelines on where reporters were allowed to file, and once again, impressed on the gaggle of journalists the rule that had been imposed from the outset:

NO LIVE TWEETING.

Carol McKinley, from *ABC*, hinted that something seemed to be brewing, and implied she expected an "explosive day." She slyly referenced the Judge indicating the prosecution's desire to put "out of town witnesses" on the stand. That could mean only one thing, and since no one was going to say it, I did. I tweeted early on Wednesday morning, before the court day got into full swing:[53]

"I'm wondering whether a full day has been set aside for the prosecution's star witness #KrystalKenney to testify. Will that be today?"

It was. But the state didn't call Kenney to the stand first. Instead, they précised her testimony with a brief introduction into the merits of Kenney's story, via FBI Special Agent Kevin Hoyland.

---

53 The timestamp refers to 17:34 GMT which was 08:34 in Colorado.

#7 HOYLAND[54]

If Kevin Hoyland's name rings a bell, it's because Hoyland was tasked with the same meticulous analysis of the cell phone narrative in the Watts case. In fact it was Hoyland who authored the comprehensive – and damning – Phone Data Review, which appears as a sort of appendix to the 1960 page discovery, when it should really be its opening chapter.

It was Hoyland's work in the Frazee case that basically allowed the breakthrough with Kenney to happen. If they knew Kenney was involved, they didn't know how involved without the Phone Data Review. Using the Phone Data Review they could question Kenney, and if her story didn't line up [or stand up to scrutiny], prosecutors and law enforcement could confidently accuse Kenney of being a hostile witness. By the same token, if Kenney co-operated, her story and the Phone Data Review ought to be a match, and if it was, that could be very good for the prosecution's case.

Early on when Hoyland was sharing his testimony, one of the journalists present [Sam Kraemer] described "an insane amount of detail" proving how Frazee's phone and Kelsey's phone travelled for extended periods together, after her disappearance. If Frazee had thought everything through in terms of disposing of actual remains, he'd been less careful about leaving behind invisible, digital breadcrumbs.

But it wasn't only Frazee's and Kelsey's phone that were leaving behind digital trails; Kenney's was too. Hoyland was able to follow Kenney's handset as it navigated its way from Idaho, on November 23rd, arriving in Florissant and Woodland Park on the 24th, before returning

---

54 FBI Agent Kevin Hoyland was the 21st prosecution witness to take the stand.

the way it had come [back to Idaho] on the 25th. We'll plumb through the phone narrative in more detail in a separate chapter, but the key takeout for investigators was that Kenney's phone provided her with an alibi, whereas Frazee's and Kelsey's did the opposite. The long ribbon of pings from Kenney's phone proved how far she was away from Kelsey when Kelsey was last seen, whereas Frazee's tangled ribbon [tangled with Kelsey's phone's movements] indicated just how mixed up he was in Kelsey's disappearance. If both of them had Kelsey's blood on their hands, the Phone Data Review showed one had a lot more blood – warm blood – on his person, than the other.

Hoyland was also able to demonstrate just how many calls, and how often Frazee called Kenney on Thanksgiving evening, and into the next day. It's as a result of this activity that prosecutors asked Frazee's brother Sean if they noticed him constantly on his phone when he arrived home after 17:00 on Thanksgiving. Sean's answer was that he didn't see Frazee on his phone, but that Frazee stepped out to do chores, and to feed the horses. Well, the *chores* were summoning Kenney. The *horse he was feeding* was Kenney.

During Hoyland's PowerPoint presentation, he indicated how tracking a cell phone's movements through a cellular network where there is mountainous terrain isn't necessarily straightforward. In this sense, Pike's Peak and Colorado's topography in general could have played havoc with the timeline, especially if Kenney [or some other accomplice] simply lived nearby. Interestingly, Verizon records only pick up Call Detail Records [CDRs] related to calls [not texts]. As recently as 2018, a US Supreme Court ruled that CDRs are so accurate, they can be regarded as the same as tracking devices [basically the surveillance tech used for espionage and the like] and thus, for such private and potentially compromising information, require a search warrant to procure, signed by a judge.

Hoyland said his analysis only focused on a handful of towers in Teller County. This doesn't necessarily mean Hoyland's analysis was incomplete, or limited in any way, but rather points to the prototypical layout of towers in rural areas. Rural areas have fewer towers, and this crime was mostly rural in nature, especially in terms of the disposal of evidence.

Strangely, Hoyland was also able to ascertain that Kelsey's phone was on Frazee's account. Frazee may have assumed he would be able to control the data on her phone if he owned the account. Hoyland focussed his review on November 21st to November 25th across all three handsets.

Starting on the evening of November 21st, Hoyland provided a slide mapping the movements of Kelsey's phone and Frazee's phone. Both handsets were in Florissant around 21:00 on November 21st. In another slide the handsets moved together toward the Nash Ranch, about 14.6 miles from the Cripple Creek tower [and the Frazee ranch]. This move also involved a drop in elevation of 1 908 feet. Early in the morning of November 22nd, the phones moved together – away from the Nash Ranch – then in an easterly direction, and finally north toward Florissant. Finally, one of the handsets departed from the other; the single signature travelled on its own to Woodland Park, arriving at about 04:00.

Obviously while all of this was happening, Kenney's phone was hundreds of miles away, not moving much at all. Kelsey's final call was to Frazee at 12:33. It's likely she was murdered within an hour of this call. The next call made from her handset occurred on the morning of November 24th, but not by Kelsey.

Ominously, there was zero activity on either phone between 12:33 and 16:20 on November 22nd. Which tower did Frazee's phone utilize during this time? The Woodland Park tower ferried two calls to Kenney, one at 16:34 and a second at 16:37. These calls immediately followed his exit captured by Jackson's surveillance camera, as well as Frazee's call home, to say he was on his way to join them for Thanksgiving. Tellingly, as Frazee left Kelsey's home with Kaylee, but without Kelsey, Kelsey's handset went along with the ride. When Frazee's handset travelled up Highway 24 and connected in Divide, Kelsey's went the same way. When it attempted to connect to a tower near Florissant at 16:40, 40 seconds later Kelsey's phone did the same.

Later on that same evening the Frazee Ranch landline called Kenney's phone. That conversation lasted 47 minutes. At 22:00 that night, Frazee's and Kelsey's phones were on the move again. After Hoyland was dismissed, Judge Sells took the court through the reasons why he closed the court on Tuesday afternoon. It was to discuss motions, legal arguments and discussion regarding upcoming witnesses. Sells repeated his concerns about privacy given the publicity of the case. It was done, Sells emphasized, to protect the integrity of the jury. And with that, the court went into recess. When the reporters emerged, one of them – Ashley Franco – tweeted that <u>the attorneys were meeting privately again</u> to address privacy concerns for an upcoming witness.

These private meetings <u>had to be about one person</u>; the person everyone was waiting to hear from except Patrick Frazee.

Krystal Kenney Takes the Stand

"What they did not tell you is that Krystal did not go to police voluntarily. They had to track her down." — Ashley Porter, legal counsel for Patrick Frazee

Hoyland, having done his job in making Kenney's alibi explicit, the prosecution called their star witness [and Achilles heel] to the stand.

#8 KENNEY[55]

At 11:00 the prosecution made the announcement everyone was expecting, and Frazee was dreading. <u>Reporters described Kenney as appearing tense.</u> According to *Fox 21* Frazee acknowledged his ex *by staring her down as she entered the courtroom.* Besides Frazee's dark eyes glaring at her, Kenney had good reason to be nervous. Her life was on the line, his life was on the line, and if she wasn't careful, what she said in court might add or subtract a year or more of her freedom.

Jennifer Viehman, the Lead Prosecutor asked Kenney to describe her backstory. Kenney, dressed in a collared shirt and sweater, her hair tied in a braid, said she grew up in Idaho, and had recently[56] moved to Hansen, Idaho.

---

55 Krystal Kenney was the 22nd prosecution witness to take the stand.

56 Kenney moved to Hansen, Idaho in early 2019. In other words, she moved shortly after becoming a key suspect in a murder investigation.

Kenney said she met Frazee when she was 20 at the Teller County Fair. At the time she was working at a guest ranch. She was clearly smitten with Frazee then, describing him as handsome, tall, all in all a "pretty good dude." So much for women's intuition, eh? Turns out he was pretty bad; the worst.

It seems Frazee and Kenney hit it off big time that year. In 2006 she went down to visit him ten times that first year – *she* visiting *him*. They chatted on the phone virtually every day. They went on trips together over weekends – Kenney was in nursing school at the time. Kenney admitted she was working three or four part-time jobs, putting herself through school. Clearly the many trips down to see Frazee weren't helping her expense account, and nor was he. Even then Kenney noticed Frazee would sometimes pull a disappearing act. Despite driving down to see him as often as she was, he sometimes didn't call her for days on end. Her last visit, coinciding with the end of the first phase of their dalliance, occurred in August 2007.

<u>The Denver Channel</u> describes a strange denouement to their almost year-long romance:

That month [August], [Frazee] asked [Kenney] to go pick up some "things" for him on his property and while she did so, she said it was "not pleasant." This was not expanded upon.

Why the heck didn't anybody – including the jury – ask about this? Consider the parallels in 2007 to what transpired 11 years and two months later:

[Frazee] asked [Kenney] to go pick up some "things" for him VS *You've got a mess to clean up.*

[She had to go to] his property and while she did so, she said it was "not pleasant." VS Going to sort out "his property" [his fiancé] in a scheme that wasn't pleasant.

Whatever the exact nature of this "unpleasantness", Kenney broke things off with Frazee for a time. He would call her and she'd ignore him. But eventually she caved, and their friendship continued, though at a slower pace than previously.

It didn't take long for Kenney to jump ship after that incident – whatever it was. In September 2007 Kenney started dating another dude, another rancher. It led to a long term relationship, culminating in Kenney become engaged to Chad Lee less than two years later, in July 2010. Kenney married Chad two months after getting engaged, on October 2nd 2010.

Throughout Kenney's romance with Chad, Frazee was in the background. Kenney said she gave Frazee the password to her voicemail, which meant Frazee knew about Chad. In court Kenney couldn't say why she gave Frazee her voicemail password. She guessed it was either simply because he asked for it, or because Kenney wanted to assure Frazee – even in her new situation – that she was loyal to him regardless. There may have been an ulterior motive. Kenney may have wanted Frazee to be jealous, and to act on that jealousy. If this was a ploy, it worked.

As mentioned previously, Frazee contacted Kenney in December 2008 just over a year into her relationship with Chad. Frazee said he wanted to give Kenney a Border Collie pup. Even then, Kenney had to go down to Colorado to fetch the animal herself. When she was down there, Frazee confronted her about the relationship. She told Frazee to make a choice between himself and Chad. Kenney may have chosen

Frazee, except she said she knew he was dating another woman [a situation that remained in place even when Kelsey disappeared].

Kenney became tearful on the witness stand as she acknowledged she still had feelings for Frazee in spite of her relationship with another man. Moreover, Frazee knew it, and was trying to pressure her into dumping Chad. Frazee spelled it out bluntly, telling Kenney:

"You can't ride two horses at the same time, so you need to make a choice."

Kenney wept in court as she admitted she'd never felt chemistry with a man like she did with Frazee.[57] Frazee set an ultimatum for Kenney. She was to break things off with Chad by March 2009. But Kenney didn't break things off. And Chad knew about Frazee when he started dating Kenney. In April, when Kenney still hadn't met his ultimatum, Frazee was pissed. He called and demanded payment for the puppy he'd given her as a gift four months earlier. When Kenney baulked, Frazee called again in May, enraged. He told Kenney if she didn't send him the money for the dog, he'd drive up to Idaho and kill the dog.

Through this limited anecdote we see how quickly Frazee becomes emasculated when he doesn't get his way. We also see how a gift is withdrawn when he has a change of heart, and it becomes a kind of political football, or punching bag, to kick down the road. In the scenario with Kelsey, his own child would be the political football, but for reasons that will be made clear, Frazee couldn't kill his child to pick up the check. It was the other way round. *He needed the child to pick up*

---

57 This statement about Kenney's chemistry with Frazee echoes what Watts said about Kessinger:

Watts said he never felt the same way about anyone in his lifetime as he did about her. – Discovery Documents, page 600

the check. Instead he would kill the child's mother, so that he could get the child, keep the child and [at least in theory] get the check.

When Frazee threatened to kill her dog, Kenney started crying over the phone. Kenney never sent him the money; Chad found out about the situation and set his own ultimatum. If she sent Frazee the money he [Chad] would be done with her [Kenney]. The dog killing conversation essentially spelled the end of her affair with Frazee. For a spell, at least.

A year passed. Then, on October 1st, 2010 Frazee called Kenney and left a voicemail asking her not to marry Chad. Her wedding was the next day. Frazee undertook to come and *rescue her* if she changed her mind. Through this simple scenario we see how manipulative Frazee is, how he plays mind games waiting until the exact moment to spring his psychological traps.

Kenney didn't fall for them, but the timing of his final ploy weighed on her. She married Chad, but she felt conflicted afterwards, second-guessing herself. She knew she'd made the right choice in sticking with Chad, but she also knew in her heart <u>she was still in love with the tall, handsome rancher</u> from Colorado. Whenever there was an unhappy moment in her marriage, her thoughts turned to Frazee. What if she'd taken him up on his offer? Could her life have turned out *differently*? Could her life have turned out *better*? As time wore on, she found herself with Frazee's dog on her lap, daydreaming increasingly of another life – a better life – with *him*.

Kenney wept on the stand, and Frazee looked down at his shoes.

Time passed. One year, then three. One time their paths crossed at the National Western Stock Show, held every January in Denver Colorado. The purpose of the exhibition is to showcase better breeding and cattle feeding techniques. It was the first time the pair had seen each other in five years. The electricity was still there.

In 2013 or 2014 Kenney heard occasionally from Frazee. A text here and a text there. She asked Frazee how he was doing. He asked her about her life. Kenney had given birth to a son in 2012, a daughter in 2014. When Kenney mentioned her daughter's name, Frazee glanced back up at Kenney. [He had a daughter too]. In 2015, five years into her marriage, Kenney and Frazee spoke for the first time over the phone. Kenney was at a nursing conference in Texas and Frazee told her to keep in touch, and that he'd love to hear from her. From then on the star-crossed lovers started communicating more and more frequently.

Kenney contrived a trip to see family and friends in Colorado, and so, in 2015 they met up again. Frazee invited her to look at his cattle, and the pair met at a gas station in Florissant as part of that arrangement. All of this – the secret trip to Colorado, the innuendo surrounding secret meetings in order to look at cattle – was really a premise to do other, more carnal things. And when they happened, Kenney said:

"It was like nothing had changed – still the same giddy feeling."

Frazee said he still felt the same way too. Frazee added that both of them had grown up some in the interim. This was an ironic statement to make. Kenney had grown up as a mother and a wife, whereas Frazee had simply continued as a bachelor, even something of a deadbeat. His decision to commit murder also shows how little he had evolved as a human being throughout his twenties and early thirties. Having said that, Kenney's decision to participate in some capacity shows how even being married, even having children, doesn't necessarily qualify one as a complete human being. In contrast, if one is married and has children and yet cheats throughout, this illustrates the capacity she had for being an incomplete individual, which is to say a broken or dysfunctional person.

Between October 2015 and 2016 Frazee and Kenney conducted an affair. Frazee pressed Kenney to get a divorce. As early as February 2016 Kenney got hold of a divorce attorney. The attorney put together the requisite documentation, and Kenney told Frazee about what was happening. Frazee encouraged her to continue, convincing her that she was "the one who got away." While this was music to Kenney's ears, it was difficult for her to believe Frazee wouldn't cheat on her. In the end, Kenney didn't file the papers.[58] And then a month later Kenney fell pregnant with a third child. Frazee was the child's father.

---

58 This not filing of legal papers is mirrored in Frazee himself drawing up custody papers but not going through with the actual legal process. Both processes were possibly avoided due to the potential costs involved.

~

"I guess you're a baby killer or you're not."

"I believe every abortion is a tragedy."
— Diane Abbott

Frazee wanted Kenney to leave her husband, and be with him, but the litmus test to that was the pregnancy. Frazee didn't pass that test. He told Kenney:

"I guess you're a baby killer or you're not."

This showed not only did he not hold life in high regard [even his own blood], but he clearly didn't hold Kenney in high regard either. And he'd put her into a really awkward situation. Now she was pregnant, and married, and what's more, he didn't want his own child. If that were true, how would he want to be married? Surely wanting the child would be part of wanting "the one that got away" and all that went with that sentiment?

Of course, it takes two to tango. Kenney had also put herself in an awkward situation. And ominously, she answered Frazee's rhetorical question by having an abortion.

"I guess you're a baby killer or you're not."

Both Frazee and Kenney were complicit not only in the tryst that led to the conception of the child, but also in the secret murder of their unborn baby. So much for Frazee and Kenney having grown up and become mature human beings. If their love had matured, why not get divorced and get married? Why create this mess? Possibly both Kenney and Frazee were hamstrung by finances. Maybe they wanted to get together, but economics were holding them back. Still, millions of couples face the same difficulties and are able to overcome them.

Kenney's decision to kill her own child, and Frazee's complicity in this [however direct or indirect[59]] provided a kind of dry run for what followed three short years later. No matter how they spun it to others, there was no way to unspin it to themselves. Rightly or wrongly, they had blood on their hands. And no one knew about it. And so – who cared?

Kenney went ahead and filed for divorce in May 2016. Evidently Kenney thought she would be exchanging one husband for her dreamboat, but the abortion was a warning flag Kenney had failed to heed. Perhaps by lying to him and saying there was a miscarriage, Kenney was counting on Frazee not having misgivings, drama or doubt about starting a new life with her. In any event, no new life materialized.

According to Kenney, Frazee "had no reaction" to her divorce. In fact, they didn't talk again for a year and a half. In October 2017, roughly a year before Frazee would recruit Kenney into his homicidal scheme, Frazee texted Kenney a strange message asking her if she still liked her children. He followed this charming gambit with a phone call. The pair chatted for two hours. During that 120 minute conversation

---

59 According to Kenney, she led Frazee to believe she'd had a miscarriage. Whether or not this is true, Frazee himself clearly indicated that he was okay with Kenney having an abortion, and in this sense, he consented to it.

Frazee forgot to mention he was in a relationship with someone else, and his daughter Kaylee had been born on October 5th, earlier that same month. In fact, Frazee's comment about Kenney's children, and his last message to Kenney, if anything, confirmed Frazee's contempt for children and the institution of marriage. Frazee didn't seem to know what he wanted. When he got what he wanted he didn't want it anymore. He was always *wanting*, never happy, and this was one of those times.

Six months later, [six months after Kaylee's birth, and six months after his call to Kenney], in March 2018, Kenney drove down to Colorado again. Kenney said they met up "to shoe horses" and "to look at land." They went out to dinner. Frazee forgot to mention anything about Kelsey or Kaylee, according to Kenney. Kenney doesn't mention whether they were intimate on this occasion, but given she was back in Colorado three months later, at the end of June [around the time Frazee stopped paying child support to Kelsey], it makes sense that something sexual was sparking again between them.

On this occasion Kenney helped Frazee "fix a fence." While they were at it, Frazee said how nice it would be to have a son around to help out.[60] When Kenney needed to blow her nose, Frazee offered her a baby wipe. Kenney said she didn't register at the time where he got it, or what it might mean. This is an odd statement to recollect to the court, because it registered enough to remember it more than a year

---

60 This reference to "wanting a son" has interesting parallels to the Watts case. His third child was going to be a boy, and Watts had always wanted a boy. But his mistress felt she was always going to come second, and hoped she might give him a son one day. This seemed to inspire Watts with the idea not only of preventing his son from being born, but ultimately wiping out his whole family.

later. Also, we've heard how Kenney is prone to sniffing. It's possible Frazee handed her more than one wipe during her visits that year. It also raises the question: did they engage in any *other* activities besides sex?

Kenney told the court she found out Frazee was a father to a little girl when she went out to dinner with a former boss. This resonates. It's more or less the same way Amber Frey[61] [Scott Peterson's mistress] found out he was married, and that his wife Laci was almost 9 months pregnant. Kenney says when she heard Frazee was a dad *her jaw hit the floor*.

---

61 <u>A work colleague of Scott Peterson told Amber's friend Shawn Sibley that Peterson was married</u>, and his wife pregnant. Shawn then told Amber, and demanded that Peterson explain to her what was going on. When he did, Peterson lied saying he was married, but that his wife had recently died. This was in early December, a few days before she disappeared.

"Kelsey likes caramel macchiatos..."

"People go missing every day..." — Patrick Frazee to Krystal Kenney

If the morning session wasn't earth shaking, it nevertheless lay the necessary and much-needed foundation for Kenney's participation in the crime [which she dealt with explicitly, and to a series of gasps from the gallery] in the afternoon session.

Why – when Kenney was asked to – did she clean up Frazee's mess? Why? True Crime Rocket Science predicts a deep psychological scar, a deep wound is necessary, to set in motion this sort of dark clandestine collaboration. Did Kenney experience that wound from Kelsey, directly? Well, yes and no. Kelsey didn't do anything – knowingly – against Kenney. But it was easy for Kenney to feel that she had, especially with Frazee whispering over her shoulder, and into her ear.

Kenney said she didn't "verbalize" her surprise when she found out Frazee was a father [KAPOW] to a little girl [KAPOW] and involved with <u>an attractive flight instructor</u> from Washington [KAPOW KAPOW] who'd moved to Colorado to be with her dream man [KAPOW KAPOW KAPOW].

If no one was aware Kenney and Frazee were an item again, or about to become one again, <u>she – Kenney – certainly was</u>. If no one was aware of his *betrayal*, asking her to kill her child while siring a child with someone else, *she* was aware of it. And *surprise* wasn't the operative word, or emotion. If she felt betrayed by him, betrayed for being lured into divorcing her own husband, abandoning – to a degree – her own family, and her own family life, then she felt bristling **resentment** for *this woman* who had stolen everything from her.

Frazee had to know how Kenney felt about the whole situation. And as his feelings changed about his fiancé, and as his feelings changed about the utility his child might have in bolstering his inheritance [as long as he could win custody], Kenney's role in Frazee's homicidal rodeo might become useful to him.

In her own version of events, uttered in court on Day 4, Kenney said she took the news on the chin. She sucked it up and swallowed it. But it festered in her stomach. She couldn't sleep. Couldn't get over it. She wanted to know who this *interloper* was who'd stolen her man, who'd stolen her shot at giving him a child. Who'd pulled the rug out from under her? <u>Who was she?</u>[62]

And so, without the implied marriage proposal from Frazee [associated with petitioning her to divorce Chad, which she had], and the obligation that sort of flowed around Kenney falling pregnant with

---

62 Frazee himself played a role in dehumanizing Kelsey. When he mentioned her to Kenney, and he did, often, he always referred to her as "<u>the mother of my child</u>." These terms of reference not only made Kelsey seem not like a person, but worse, triggered Kenney in the worst possible way. Kenney was forced to think of Kelsey in the way that was most painful to her: the mother of his child meant she was a rival, one who'd stolen her man, stolen her shot at happiness. By helping Frazee commit the crime, and cover it up, Kenney figured through an emotional fugue, that she could get her comeuppance on her rival, and win her dream man back. It was yet another opportunity for her to prove her loyalty to her man, and win her way back into the center of his life.

his child [associated with petitioning her to get rid of their child, which she had], was this grating juxtaposition: there was another woman he was in a serious relationship with, <u>and they'd had a child together</u>.

Kenney's response was a mixture of horror and fascination, anger and that sickening self-destructive curiosity that turns ordinary people into stalkers, and their own worst enemies. Frazee could work with that, and he did, didn't he?

Kenney was back in Colorado in August to "load horses" and to ride one of them. During this sojourn on the Frazee ranch, Kenney made her feelings known to the rancher in a way that suited her best. She handed him a bag of baby items while telling him, "I know." Frazee took the gesture – the accusation – in his stride. He played for time. He told Kenney, "Now isn't the time to talk about it." Kenney hoped he would talk about it eventually. He owed her that much.

In early September Frazee sent Kenney a photo of Kaylee. By this time the plan was already lodged inside Frazee's mind. He saw the whole drama unfolding perfectly in a series of acts. He saw it all from beginning to end. He could get rid of a bunch of birds with one stone. He could use Kenney to get rid of Kelsey, and then get rid of Kenney whenever he wanted to. In court, Kenney reflected that she felt – in hindsight – what Frazee was doing, what he was achieving with her… she used the slang term "pawn".

According to *The Denver Channel*:

[Kenney] said she felt she was being "pawned" [by Frazee]…

The conventional dictionary meaning doesn't do that word justice, nor is it strictly speaking the precise word or meaning Kenney is angling at here. In fact the apposite term is *pwn*, a slang term derived from the word *own*, where something or someone is appropriated or conquered.

It implies domination and humiliation. It's used often in Internet-based video game culture to taunt an opponent who has just been defeated. Kenney's use of this slang term says something about her background, and for that matter, Frazee's. It suggests they inhabited some kind of subculture where different rules, and different terms apply.

Kenney is 100% spot on in the use of this word to describe her situation. The key fact is that when she was *pwned* she didn't know it. But he did.

Kenney testified that Frazee kept her in the dark about the "true nature" of his relationship with Kelsey. Probably he didn't tell her the same story he'd told Kelsey, that got her to move halfway across America to be with him. Instead, Frazee told a story about an abusive mother. It's unlikely Kenney believed this story. She suggested he report Kelsey to child protective services. Frazee said he had. Kenney never noticed any signs of abuse. More likely, from the way Frazee was running Kelsey down, Kenney was less interested in the veracity of Frazee's claims, and more stimulated by the knowledge that Frazee was unhappily ensconced in his relationship. If he wanted out, well then Kenney didn't mind helping out. Getting Kelsey out the picture, whether she was a good mom or not, whether she was abusing Kaylee or not, probably mattered less to Kenney than getting someone out of the way so that she could get back into the picture with Frazee.

Frazee's first ploy was to use Kenney's nursing *nous* to get rid of Kelsey for good. Frazee's idea was for Kenney to poison Kelsey's favorite drink, then offer it to her as part of a gesture of friendship, gratitude or support. Kenney said if "someone" mixed <u>Valium and Ambien</u>, and gave it to Kelsey, it could do some permanent damage.[63]

---

63 A moderately high dose of Ambien and Valium can be lethal.

According to Kenney, she "already had plans" to go to a birthday party in Greeley Colorado, at the time the first murder plot was hatched and, as such, she'd be around to possibly execute this plan when push came to shove. Frazee told Kenney about Kelsey's favorite drink, and the idea materialized of a drug cocktail that would end the impasse with her.

As part of his psychological manipulation, Frazee reasoned to Kenney:

"People go missing every day."

Moreover, Frazee made a compelling argument. He told Kenney that Kelsey was already struggling with alcohol, drugs and depression. And so if she died of an overdose, or even if she simply disappeared, no one would be suspicious.

In theory this idea made sense. So, after the birthday party in Greeley, Kenney headed directly to Woodland Park. According to Kenney she had her aunt drive her to Kelsey's home, possibly using the same ruse she used when she returned to the same spot weeks later in a friend's borrowed black VW Passat. As long as she pitched up in a vehicle that wasn't hers, how could anyone link her to Kelsey?[64]

In Kenney's own words, she wanted to "swing by" to see a friend in Woodland Park. In reality, she didn't want to swing by, Frazee wanted her to swing by. What she wanted was the same thing he wanted.

"He wanted her [Kelsey] not to be a problem anymore."

These words used in court – swing by – reveal just how familiar Kenney had become in the year following the bludgeoning. They are words that relate to the murder itself when it was finally and fatefully

---

64 Like Frazee, Kenney didn't seem very familiar with modern law enforcement methods as regards cell phone tracking.

executed, and the murder weapon, which we'll deal with in a moment. In Kenney's frame of reference here, Kelsey wasn't beaten to death, Kenney sees Kelsey's death more a matter of someone *swinging by*. Swinging was involved, clearly, but it's hardly as innocent or as innocuous as Kenney's minimizing words imply.

Kenney arrived at Woodland Park after dark, at around 21:00. Kenney said Kelsey appeared "guarded." Good for her. Interestingly, Kenney became emotional as she spoke in court, in front of a packed gallery, about this first-hand encounter with Kelsey. According to *The Denver Channel*:

[Kenney] didn't want to hurt [Kelsey] and [she] hoped Frazee would be relieved nothing happened to her.

This is hard to believe. If Kenney didn't want to hurt Kelsey herself, why was she there? Why was she there with the coffee, as instructed? Why was she there with a caramel macchiato, as instructed? Why *wouldn't* she be there with a spiked drink?

Kenney's emotions at this point with the court feels like an attempt to curry sympathy with the public, especially the reporters present. It makes absolutely no sense that Frazee "would be relieved" nothing had happened to Kelsey, nor that Kenney honestly thought Frazee would feel that way. No surprise then, when he called the next morning once she was on her way back to Idaho [boy, she'd gotten herself out of Dodge pretty quick, hadn't she?] he "aggressively" interrogated her on what had happened. Frazee must have called Kelsey first and been disappointed that she'd answered her phone, then called Kenney to demand an explanation. Kenney's explanation was that Kelsey probably didn't drink the spiked coffee. This is likely accurate.

<u>Did Kenney spike Kelsey's drink?</u> We have no way of knowing for sure, but what we do know for sure is Kelsey told her colleagues about an awkward moment when a stranger arrived at her door, and gave her coffee. We don't know whether Kelsey drank it, but one can imagine if she had she would've felt poorly at a minimum, and since she didn't, Kelsey probably didn't drink the coffee, or if she did, didn't drink all of it.

Is it more likely Kenney spiked Kelsey's drink, or more likely she didn't? The best predictor of the future is the past, and vice versa. We know what followed Kenney giving Kelsey the macchiato. We know Frazee made additional requests to Kenney, and Kenney never told Frazee to go to hell which is why he kept pestering her with one scheme after another. We also know Frazee felt he could rely on Kenney sufficiently that, having finally committed the murder, he was comfortable to exit the scene having left plenty of evidence to clean up. When he asked Kenney to clean up his mess, he *knew* she would. And he was right – she did.

Kenney getting her hands dirty with Kelsey's blood, and a fragment of her teeth, and being there when her body was burned corresponds with <u>Kenney participating in spiking the Starbucks coffee</u>. But death by poisoning is hardly an exact science. Chris Watts evidently tried the same thing with Shan'ann. We know she felt poorly on a few occasions, and each failed attempt taught her killer about a more "effective" dose.

After the botched coffee incident, it wasn't long before Frazee hatched another plan.

"Make sure there's not a lot of blood..."

"I'll give you one more chance to redeem yourself." — Patrick Frazee to Krystal Kenney, according to Kenney

Krystal Kenney told a packed courtroom, hanging on her every word, that she didn't tell the police about Frazee's plots and plans because *she was hoping it would just go away*. But Frazee didn't just go away, and neither did Kelsey. And even though the problem recurred, and the plots recurred [and the so the problem wasn't going away], Kenney persisted in not going to the authorities. [She did the same for weeks after the crime was committed, and despite massive media coverage wanting to know what had happened, and where this woman had disappeared to, even then, Kenney knew, but wasn't going to tell, not voluntarily].

I wish it would just go away.

It's likely true that Kenney did want "it" to just go away, the "it" being the woman standing in the place of her, and once she was gone, the fact of her *being* gone.

I wish it would just go away.

Frazee felt the same way too. According to *The Gazette*, Frazee asked Kenney to kill Kelsey three times.

Frazee asked her three times to kill Berreth — first with a poisoned cup of coffee, then with a metal rod and finally with a bat, she told the jury. Each time, he instructed her to just "swing away," Lee recalled.

More accurately, Frazee asked Kenney four times, and Kenney only acted on three of the requests. The first involved the coffee in early October, the second involved a pipe on October 15th, the third attempt was the next night – October 16th – and finally on November 4th, three weeks prior to the murder, Frazee called her and appealed to her one final time. Kenney was in the car with family, she claimed, and couldn't talk to Frazee. Frazee called back half an hour later. He had a simple message for her:

"It's time."

Frazee knew she knew what he was talking about. She didn't need to be informed, or convinced. The idea was already internalized in her heart and her mind.

Kenney made some effort to meet Frazee half way, or to be accurate, all the way. She looked at available flights, but they were too expensive. Kenney's reasoning seems absurd if it's true.

I can't afford to come down and kill Kelsey, otherwise I would do it.

If it is true, then one can see how both Frazee and Kenney were in the same bind – they were both struggling financially. We have no idea whether Kenney expected to profit in some specific way from her involvement, or whether she knew or anticipated how Frazee expected to benefit – materially – from Kelsey's death, and gaining automatic custody [in theory] of Kaylee. What we do know is having just divorced her husband, Kenney ought to have been familiar with the costs of taking a spouse to court, arguing over alimony and the difficulties of child support.

Incredibly, Frazee seemed to expect her to drive all the way down from Idaho for the umpteenth time, confront Kelsey on his behalf, and kill her – for Kaylee's sake. And she was expected to do it simply because Frazee had asked. In the same way that prosecutors were dumbfounded when discussing Watts' motive in court, wondering why he couldn't simply get a divorce, one wonders how Kenney failed to rationalize a raft of other possibilities. Besides calling child services, if she really believed Kaylee was in danger [which is hard to believe], Kenney could have called Kelsey herself and told her Frazee wanted her gone. Kenney had to have known this wasn't an option, because with Kelsey gone, Kaylee would be too, and he [or perhaps they] needed Kaylee to be part of the equation.

Curiously, Kenney referred to Frazee balling in his truck, telling her at one point she would have to take Kaylee. What this suggests is that:

1) Frazee didn't see himself actually *exercising* custody over Kaylee, even if he got official custody of his child.

2) If it's true that he saw a role for Kenney in a sort of foster mother role for Kaylee, the possibility of her sharing in some kind of material way, possibly in an inheritance stipend intended for Frazee if he had custody of Kaylee, may have factored into her motive.

Frazee also assured Kenney that killing "isn't that hard", adding that other friends of his would do it but they couldn't because they were too close to the situation. It sounds as if Kenney came fairly close to executing the second request – with the pipe. Just like she did with the coffee, she actually drove to Kelsey's home, and waited. She staked the place out. She knew Kaylee wasn't home, so she only had Kelsey to deal with. Woman vs Woman. While she sat there she heard Frazee's cajoling playing through her mind.

"It isn't that hard. It really isn't that hard. People disappear all the time."

She held the pipe in her hand. Then put it aside. Then picked it up again.

"It isn't that hard. It really isn't that hard."

To her credit, Kenney wasn't convinced. Murder *is* hard. The word itself is used as a noun sometimes to describe something that's extremely difficult, perilous or unpleasant.

...driving around London is murder...
That final exam was murder!

And people don't disappear all the time. Kenney didn't simply abandon her post, she wrestled with her mission until exhaustion took over. She slept rough that night, in a gas station. Whether an opportunity presented itself or not, or whether Kenney failed to find her "courage", whichever it was, Kenney eventually bailed and headed back to her master. Her master wasn't pleased.

Kenney spent the day on the Frazee Ranch babysitting Kaylee. She'd failed to kill Kaylee's mother on her father's orders, but she'd get another chance at the end of the day's babysitting. When Frazee arrived home he criticized Kenney in terms of chores and odd jobs she'd done in his absence. It was then, Kenney claimed [with some justification] that she realized Kelsey was probably "innocent" after all.

Despite this insight, this revelation, Frazee recruited Kenney into his third murderous plot in two weeks. Frazee told Kenney *she had one more chance* [for what? to win the inheritance lottery? to woo her way back into his bed?] and he offered Kenney an effective tool to that end. Frazee asked Kenney if she had a bat. We know Frazee had a few wooden baseball bats at home. Frazee handed her a bat. It was an improvement on the pipe. Frazee, perhaps subconsciously <u>channelling a line out of the movie *SIGNS*</u>, told Kenney to <u>take the bat and "swing away."</u>

Kenney, with her murder weapon on hand, drove to Kelsey's townhome a third time. For a second time in two attempts she got out of her car and waited. [No mention is made of where the bat was during this third sojourn to the chocolate brown townhome in Woodland Park.]

Meanwhile, Kelsey and Frazee exchanged Kaylee [which implies Kaylee would be present when Kelsey arrived home, just as she was when Frazee killed Kelsey himself the following month]. Kenney dabbed her eyes with a tissue as she addressed the court on this aspect of her story. Once again, it feels like a special plea for sympathy. She's off – for a third time – to bludgeon her rival, but she's the victim.

"It's going to be her or me."

Not if she went to cops right then. Or the next day, or for the next thirty days. Or for the next sixty days. Of course, if she had gone to the cops right then, ironically, she may have been nailed for a far more serious crime [attempted murder perhaps] than the one she was ultimately charged with [tampering with a crime scene].[65]

---

65 Kenney wasn't even charged with the more serious form of tampering: <u>tampering with a deceased human body</u>. This charge can result in a sentence of four to twelve years, potentially far more than the maximum three years Kenney is faced with [at the time of writing].

It's not clear how long Kenney waited for her victim to arrive. As it happened, Kenney lost her nerve, and drove back to Florissant. She passed Kelsey on the way.

"It's going to be her or me."

If Kenney had let herself off the hook, she wasn't going to let Kelsey off the hook too, which would have been easy to do. All she had to do was tell Kelsey. Problem was, Kelsey could tell the cops about the coffee incident, and then Kenney would be in real trouble.

When Kenney joined Frazee she told him not only could she not kill Kelsey, she *wouldn't*. She was adamant. Frazee took Kenney's obstinacy in his stride.

"If something happens to Kaylee it'll be your fault…"

Frazee's threats didn't end there. Frazee told her her ex-husband was a great dad and would be fine on his own. The import of this was obvious. Frazee was suggesting if Kenney didn't do his bidding, *she* might disappear.

"People go missing every day."

Frazee got out the car and slammed the door.

BAM.

The shit just got real.

Accessory

"That which does not kill us makes us stronger." —
Friedrich Nietzsche

Friedrich Nietzsche's comment about what doesn't kill us makes us stronger has dubious import in true crime, where it's less about surviving death, than killers finding their own paths of least resistance. When Frazee slammed the door shut, he turned back to Kenney and wagged his finger at her.

"Put her body in a garbage can, take her to Idaho and [snarling now] figure something out."

If what had gone on before were a series of veiled threats, the veil was lifted now. Either you do this, or you're going to get it.

In the court room, Frazee stared down at the floor as Kenney described the incident.

Kenney drove back to Idaho. No matter how far she got, it didn't feel like she could get away from this. She didn't want to think about it, and yet she kept thinking about it. She didn't want to be in, and yet was in the thick of it. What was really going on in her psychology, and his? The True Crime Rocket Science diagnosis is simple. Kenney and Frazee were locked in a bind of commitment and control, and that bind was escalating into criminal intent. Frazee wanted Kenney to prove her commitment, but he also needed to control her in every conceivable way or this thing could blow up in his face. Kenney *wanted* to prove her commitment, just not like this. She *wanted* to give Frazee some control, just not like this, and not everything. She needed to keep a few aces in her pocket.

On the long drive to Idaho his words circled in her head like ravens through a cloudy sky. They flapped back and forth in her brain, beating loudly in her ears. Her icy blue eyes blinked as the road wound through endless miles of dark pine forest. Kenney thought about the diminutive figure she'd handed the macchiato to. And Kaylee, the little girl who should have been *their* little girl. And Frazee himself, recently fatherless, and about to receive his inheritance, his comeuppance.

"It's going to be her or me."

Three weeks later Frazee called but Kenney blew him off. He called again. She blew him off again. If he wanted this done, he needed to do it. But she'd help clean up the mess. She'd cover for him. Well, that was something.

Commitment and control. Victim versus perpetrator. Which one was it gonna be? Which was Kenney going to be? She didn't want to be anyone's victim.

And so *"It's going to be her or me"* had evolved to *"It's going to be me or you."* They were in it together, they were on the same side, weren't they?

On November 21st he called again. They had a "fairly normal conversation" but really all Frazee wanted to know was whether she was still on his side or not. Was she still with him, despite everything, or not? She was. She was with him to the end.

Frazee mentioned nothing about Thanksgiving. Then, very early the next morning, November 22nd – Thanksgiving – he called again. Kenney didn't answer. He wished her a happy Thanksgiving. If he was going to do this he needed to know she was with him. He needed a fall-back plan, an exit, and a scapegoat.

It's going to be her or me.

It's going to be me or you.

Frazee also asked her to call him.

She did.

Throughout the day he called her.

Kenney was having Thanksgiving with her family. She broke away at one point, from the laughter and the feast, to hear Frazee snarling on the other end:

"Answer your FUCKING phone!"

She'd never heard him this rattled. She was terrified, and fascinated, alarmed and curious.

When she asked about her, he answered, and then she knew.

"Yeah, you've got a mess to clean up."

She'd let him down, so he had to do it. Now she had to make it up to him. This was her chance to prove her commitment, to regain control, to get back on the horse.

"How soon can you get here?"

Kenney said she wasn't sure.

"Figure it out."

Kenney said she would.

"You'd better figure it out fast."

Frazee hung up.

The next day Frazee called to find out if she had a plan. She did.[66] He complained, Kenney said in court, about Kelsey taking a while *to get him medication*. More likely Frazee complained about how long Kelsey took to die. Why would Frazee tell her about Kelsey,[67] and what he did to her? To lock Kenney in. To intimidate her. To control her. She was worried she was being set up. She was even more worried if she didn't do as he said, she was next. She owed him. And if Kenney wasn't careful *It's going to be her or me* was going to become *It's going to be her _and_ me.*

She was already in the middle of this, it was time to show her commitment. To do that she had to take control of the situation, and herself. He'd done the worst part. She just had to do one thing, the stuff she saw and did every day in the hospital, and it would be done forever. And then maybe it would all go away.

That same day Kenney changed her shift, called her friend, and exchanged cars [Kenney exchanged her car for a black VW Passat]. They swapped vehicles in the parking lot of Walmart in Jerome, Idaho. Kenney then drove home, grabbed what she needed [bleach, a hair net, globes, black garbage bags and a second set of clean clothes] and set off for Woodland Park.

---

66 Kenney claimed in court that her decision to drive down to Colorado was spontaneous. Given the speed at which she arranged another vehicle, and her availability at short notice, it shouldn't be

67 Although it's pure speculation that at this point [November 22nd] Frazee told Kenney about what he'd done to Kelsey, Kenney testified that Frazee told her in graphic detail about Kelsey's final moments. Thus, irrespective of when Frazee shared this information with her, the intention was the same: to lock her into his crime physically, emotionally and psychologically. All of this was a way to achieve the requisite commitment and control Frazee needed over the situation he'd fomented.

~

Rodeo Queen

"There were details enough to know that it [Kelsey's murder] probably did happen." — Krystal Kenney's testimony on Trial Day 4

In court, Kenney said she didn't know what the situation was with Kelsey during her drive south. At one point she said she suspected Frazee was trying to lure her down to Colorado to commit the murder. If that were true, how did she know to pack cleaning materials[68] and a hazmat suit, with no mention of murder weapons or drug cocktails? No, it seems fairly clear before Kenney left what she had been assigned to do.

Through Salt Lake, Grand Junction, Breckenridge and into Florissant, Frazee talked to her all the way down. When she stopped to fill up the car in Wellington, Frazee explained the blood he needed her to clean up was in the living room for the most part. The drive into Colorado – not Kenney's first – took all of twelve hours. Kenney had

---

68 On December 21st, bodycam footage captures Kenney on the Frazee ranch near the burn patch admitting to getting bleach from her home. Kenney also admitted to the same in court.

Call records indicate Frazee called Kenney at 07:23, 10:47, 11:39 and 17:21 on November 24th. Initially Kenney told investigators she was at the Frazee Ranch between 09:00 and 17:00 inquiring about a horse she wanted to purchase.

plenty of time to stop, to reconsider, to turn around and go home. She had time to call the cops, to call anyone and tell them what she was about to do. Especially since she was driving at night. She didn't.[69]

Kenney said she left Idaho at 18:00 and arrived very early at the Frazee Ranch, close to 06:30, or 25 minutes before sunrise. She'd collected the keys to Kelsey's townhome from his gate. She parked some distance away at the Woodland Park Cultural Center shortly after 07:00. Then, through the pale dawn light, Kenney waddled along the sidewalk with her cleaning gear. The former rodeo queen entered the crime scene knowing exactly what she needed to do:

- Clean the candles

- Sort out the bathroom

- Wipe away the bloody footprints scattered throughout the living room And one more thing:

- Look for Kelsey's tooth inside a vent

Kenney was up for all of it. When she stepped inside the room she saw blood all over the living room floor, over walls, over the furniture, splashed over appliances and a trail going upstairs. Then her phone rang. It was Frazee, he wanted to know what she thought. Did she crack a joke? Did he?

Frazee instructed her to find and clean specific items in the house. Did Kenney assure him she was on it, and that she would let him know when she was done? Kenney slipped into a painter's suit, donned rubber gloves and shoe covers, pulled on a hair net and got busy cleaning.

___

69 In late March 2021, about 18 months after *Murder Most Foul* was published, Judge Scott Sells reiterated the point that was made in this chapter. According to *KTVB* Judge Sells told Kenney:
"You had hours and hours and hundreds of miles when you drove back from Idaho to Colorado to again, do the right thing: Call law enforcement..."

Using her bottle of bleach from home, she filled up a spray bottle with parts water, parts bleach, and used rags from the bathroom to mop down and wipe up.

What couldn't be cleaned she removed. She found a blood-soaked sweater with its arms tied up. She pulled down the blood stained curtains, collected stuffed animals stained with Kelsey's blood, and an exercise ball discolored red. Kenney took special care to wipe clean a framed photo of Frazee, Kelsey and Kaylee covered in round drops of Kelsey's dried blood. Each wipe of Kelsey's bloodstains brought the three people under the smears back into view. Once it was clean, Kenney put it back in its place, as if to prove all was well with Frazee, with Kelsey and with Kaylee.

She followed large prints – made by boots –to the kitchen, up the stairs into the bedroom and into the bathroom. Just as he said, the candles were there. She cleaned these too, and then the bathroom. Then the prints made by Frazee's boots stomping through the scene. As Kenney moved, cleaned and wiped, there was just the soft sound of plastic garbage bags rustling, material wiping on walls and wood, and the former rodeo queen breathing heavily as she labored from one end of the bloodied scene to the other.

Kenney heaved the cedar chest to one side and found Kelsey's tooth. How did Frazee know it was there? He must have seen the tooth fly from Kelsey's mouth, or perhaps he kicked it while stomping across the room to get Kaylee.

According to Kenney:

"It wasn't like a can of paint thrown on the wall. It was like if you took a paintbrush and flicked paint on the wall."

In fact it wasn't about paint or paintbrushes, it was a young mother's blood splattered around her home in the most brutal and violent execution imaginable. To Kenney she wasn't cleaning up blood, but paint. These splatter marks were the result of the bat smashing repeatedly into its soft target, and also whipping backward [dripping red] and swinging back.

Kenney explained to the jury she thought she was going to be next. Yet, with her life in imminent danger, instead of fleeing the scene, Kenney did exactly as she was told. And she did it for four hours. Throughout this time Frazee called her[70] with something else he'd thought of for her to clean. Kenney told the court she had feelings of regret that she did nothing to stop Kelsey's murder. But those feelings of regret didn't stop her from covering up or putting a stop to Frazee.

Kenney assured the jury that she left "little spots" of blood intentionally because she wanted to raise suspicion about what happened. But the places she claimed she purposefully didn't clean, wasn't the place that Clint Berreth noticed – the splodge on the underside of the toilet bowl. There was also an easier way of communicating what had happened besides leaving behind almost invisible clues – she could have left an anonymous tip. But she didn't.

Instead, by the time Kenney was done mopping the floor, she'd filled six garbage bags[71] with blood-soaked rags. She took these bags outside and put them on the ground in the alley next to Kelsey's car. Then she locked Kelsey's townhome.

____

70 Two of the six garbage bags were white, the rest were black.

71 The Frazee Ranch just off Highway 24 was also along <u>the same route Kenney would have taken to return to Idaho</u>.

Kenney said she loaded the trash bags into the trunk of her car. Since she said she parked somewhere else, this suggests she drove closer to the scene. Her phone buzzed. Frazee again.

"Send me a few text messages saying you're coming to look at horses..."

Frazee told Kenney when to send them. And so she did. Feeling relieved that her morning chore was over, and hungry [it was around 11:00], Kenney headed to the Sonic drive through to get her family lunch. <u>A CCTV camera recorded the blonde woman moments after exiting the crime scene primping and playing with her hair</u>, taking a swig of water, checking her phone and basically gearing up for the next chapter of her life with her dreamboat. Did she assume – despite the blood on her hands, and the bloodbath that had just filled six garbage bags – she was going to just walk in and take the place of Kaylee's mother?

Incineration

"Love, like fire, goes out without fuel." — Mikhail Lermontov, A Hero of Our Time

From the <u>Sonic Burger Drive-In</u>, Kenney turns the nose of the black Passat <u>onto Highway 24 and heads due west</u> for the Frazee Ranch.[71]

When she arrives Frazee asks:

"Did you get it done?"

Kenney answers:

"I did the best I could do."

And she did. Can we agree, beyond the moral and ethical side of things, the nurse from Idaho executed her mission *very well*. She *did* do her best. She cleaned up so well that when the police were called to the residence, they saw nothing amiss. She did such a good job, when Kelsey's family entered the residence and occupied it, it wasn't until two to three days later that they spotted the first trace of blood.

As mentioned earlier, they didn't spot it where Kenney said she'd intentionally left it. They found blood where Kenney had *unintentionally* left blood. Very likely this blood trace was caused by the knee of Kenney's overall as she bent over the toilet cleaning, near to the end of her mopping up operation.

If Kenney did do her best then what does that say about her commitment not only to Frazee, but to his murderous scheme? If Kenney did her best, what does that say about her level of control over herself, and her sense of control over the situation? She didn't abandon the scene the moment she realized what had happened. Nor did she skip town a short while later, as second thoughts stole upon her. Nor did she, half way done, lose her nerve. No, she stayed and cleaned until it was all done. Four hours of cleaning, whether blood or dust, is a lot of work. Cleaning someone else's house is a lot of work. Cleaning up a crime scene in someone else's house for someone else is a heck of a lot of commitment, and a hell of a lot of self-control, <u>wouldn't you agree?</u>

Frazee told Kenney both their lives depended on how good a job she'd done, which is ironic in itself. If Frazee hadn't made a mess to begin with there wouldn't be a mess to clean up. As crime scenes go, Frazee's scores perhaps the highest for being the messiest. It hits the opposite end of the scale when compared to the Watts case, where not a single drop of blood was spilled. It's comparable to the bloodbaths of victims such as Nicole Brown Simpson,[72] Meredith Kercher, Teresa Halbach and Reeva Steenkamp.

This begs the question, did Frazee *want* to involve another person spending several hours at the scene? If you think about it, Kenney had a motive of her own for wanting Kelsey out of the way and Frazee knew

---

72 Because there were two victims in the Simpson case, and due to the manner of death [multiple stab wounds, including to the throat], the Simpson crime scene is comparably grotesque to the Kelsey Berreth crime scene. But given the nature of the injuries, through massive blunt force trauma, and the length of time the victim likely survived the initial battering, it's hard to imagine a more gruesome murder scene than the one Frazee left behind for Kenney to clean.

it. So perhaps a bloodbath was part of the plan. Had Kenney been able to arrive earlier, when the blood was still wet, perhaps he was counting on traces being tied to Kenney, if the cops ever figured out she'd come to harm.

After meeting up with Frazee and Kaylee, they had lunch together, and then the two discussed what had happened to Kelsey. Frazee, wiping burger juice from his mouth, told Kenney how hard it was to eat Thanksgiving dinner with his family while "the mother of your child is in a tote in the back of your truck." Frazee repeated the lie that he was worried Kelsey would harm Kaylee, and they had to stop her.

Frazee explained how the murder happened. He'd carried a baseball bat under a sweater, then got Kelsey to volunteer to be blindfolded with another sweater with the ruse of playing a "guess the scent" game using a set of scented candles.

Frazee said he'd "swung away" at Kelsey, but thought in future he'd stick to normal weapons and do things "the old fashioned way" as the baseball bat was too "inhumane." Frazee told Kenney once Kelsey was dead, he retrieved the tote from the back of his truck and carried it into Kelsey's condo. He put Berreth and the bat inside the tote, washed his pants [possibly in the washing machine] and did some cursory cleaning up.

During her testimony Kenney said she told Frazee she had to get back to Idaho, because there was a birthday party she wanted to attend. Also, her family were under the impression she hadn't left town. Now, we know Kenney left Idaho on November 23rd, arrived in the area early in the morning on the 24th and was done cleaning by around 11:00. After lunch on the 24th, what did Kenney do?[73] Well, we know she

------

73 From CCTV footage it's clear <u>Frazee went to the Conoco gas station near</u>

didn't go home immediately. Although Kenney didn't spend the night with Frazee on the Frazee Ranch during this trip, she didn't head back home immediately after the clean-up either. It does beg the question, if she had spent the night, what would have happened? Would there have been carnal relations that night? It's a fair question to ask, because it redirects our attention to motive [Kenney's motive] and issues of commitment and control. If the two did sleep together before the incident, did they sleep together after it? Because sleeping together would be a sign that both were committed to the outcome as it stood at the time, trusted one another, and had collectively assumed control over the situation. It was also potentially a symbol of the "new" family coming together, now that the old one was being done away with.

In this respect Kenney's testimony that what her family thought, and a birthday party elsewhere, were figuring on her radar given what had just happened and why, rings a little hollow, doesn't it?

On the afternoon of November 24th[th] Kenney's still in Florissant. If Kenney truly believed her life was in danger 1) she wouldn't have come down from Idaho in the first place, 2) she would have left at the first sign that Kelsey had been murdered and 3) she clearly wouldn't have stayed for lunch, and the remainder of the afternoon and early evening in Colorado.[74]

In Kenney's version of events, on the morning of November 25th[th] – a Sunday – Frazee approached her and handed her Kelsey's phone. He instructed her on the password, and told Kenney to drive back to Woodland Park where she [Kenney] would text Cheryl Berreth,

---

Florissant and filled up a red-white can of gasoline. This occurred between approximately 16:35 and 16:37 on November 24th[th].

74 Kenney departed Florissant at approximately 21:40 on November 24th[th].

pretending to be Kelsey. In the text she would tell Kelsey's mother she would call the next day, Monday the 26th.

From there Kenney returned to the Frazee Ranch. On Sunday afternoon, Frazee and Kenney headed <u>to the Nash Ranch</u> to retrieve the tote <u>from the top of a haystack</u>. Frazee used a tractor to retrieve the tote, but exactly how is not known. Kenney said she didn't look at the tote. Her precise role on the Nash Ranch is also unknown.

According to Kenney, as they drove back to the Frazee Ranch with Kelsey's remains in the tote, in the bed of the truck behind them, *Frazee started crying.*[75] He spoke about what might happen to Kaylee, and that he might need Kenney to take her. It's hard to imagine Frazee showing any remorse, but right here it seems this performance was calculated to draw Kenney's attention away from the dead body they were transporting in the back of the truck.

Commitment and control...

If the blood didn't quite make the crime feel real, the body in the back enclosed in the drippy black container, and the smell, made the hypothetical nature of what was happening right then recede. Frazee needed to get Kenney's mind off the here and now, and back to him, and Kaylee, and how she could still help them.

Commitment and control...

Frazee also told her where his cattle papers were, along with the key to his safe. All of this was designed for one purpose, to keep Kenney in the game, and to prevent her from freaking out.

Commitment and control...

---

75 It's possible this story is fictitious, and rather than Frazee crying about the situation, perhaps they were both chuckling about it.

Once back on the ranch, <u>Frazee drove a short distance further up the slope</u>, between the pine trees, <u>to the dog pens</u>. Next Frazee got out the truck and unloaded the tote, once again, apparently without any assistance from Kenney. Frazee dragged the tote <u>over sloping ground</u> and placed it in an empty water trough near the top of the gravel driveway. The biscuit-brown driveway linked the dog pens to the ranch home <u>about 200 yards away</u>. In the same area, <u>many wooden pallets</u> were scattered about and piled onto one another. *Kindling*. Kenney watched[76] as more and more kindling was added to the metal drinking trough. Incredibly, <u>it was situated in the center of a clearing</u>, within visual range from the family home [essentially on the road surface].

Next he snatched a red gas can bleached near-white by sun and weather exposure from the back of his truck. He poured gasoline over the tote and then over the bat, and Kelsey's body inside it. When Frazee <u>flipped the lid</u>, Kenney claimed she looked away,[77] or didn't look inside. Kenney said this was because she didn't want to.

---

76 In Kenney's version of events, though she actively participated in the cleaning up of the crime scene, presents herself as no more than a spectator with the transport and incineration of the body. She doesn't see anything, doesn't do much of anything [besides burying some of Kelsey's blood-soaked possessions, including her bible]

77 Given Kenney's ability to stomach the cleaning up of the crime scene, as well as being present through the scene phase of the crime [the disposal], along with the fact that she said Frazee told her in detail what had happened, it would seem probable that Kenney didn't look away. However, by saying this, she "excuses herself" from having to report on, and account for the gruesome state of the poor young woman's brutalized body. Naturally if Kenney did see for herself the extent of destruction wrought on poor Kelsey's body prior to incineration, it makes her going along with Frazee all the more sickening and unfathomable.

<u>Frazee broke off a few pieces of pallet wood</u>, placed them in a bucket and poured gasoline into the buckets. He allowed the gasoline to soak into the pieces of timber before adding them to the fire stack.

Then Frazee flicked a match onto the doused pile, a combination of plastic, pallets, gasoline and human flesh and blood. A butterfly of flame erupted into a leaping dragon. Huge flames quickly flapped into the sky, surprising both bystanders. Tall as trees they were, and bright yellow. Frazee moved quickly to drag a section of corrugated tin to subdue the flames. When the plastic began to boil and melt, velvet licks of acrid black tongues twirled through the smoke. The furnace roared, and hissed. Dry wood sparked and shot. The trough shuddered as the inferno stewed, seared and cooked.

Despite the promising kiln Frazee had created, the contents of the tote initially resisted the fire. So Frazee scavenged motor oil [possibly from the back of his truck]. Now the fire burned hotter. He tossed buckets that had formerly contained gasoline and sticks of timber onto the fire.

According to Kenney, none of the six garbage bags were burned here,[78] but the one way Kenney said she did assist Frazee was by helpfully placing Kelsey's bloodstained bible[79] into the flames. Then she added one of Kaylee's toys, also speckled with her mother's blood. Quickly it was all consumed and bubbled into the sky in a narrow column of churning smoke.

----

78 Kenney not burning the six garbage bags in a furnace designed to do precisely that also seems unlikely.

79 It's probable that the bible and toy was placed in the fire not only by Kenney, but as part of the process of burning the contents of the six garbage bags when Kenney returned to the scene in the black Passat, as the next chapter explains.

~

3 Calls from the FBI

"When she awoke, the world was on fire." — Scott Westerfeld, Uglies

While Frazee was still working to turn Kelsey's body and bones to ashes, it seems Kenney left the scene, took Frazee's truck and drove to the Conoco gas station just down the road. There she retrieved her vehicle and drove the Passat back to the ranch. It was at this point that she unloaded the six garbage bags, and placed the bible, toys and other blood-soaked paraphernalia onto the flames.

Once the fire work was done, a black burn patch of <u>melted plastic and melted human remains</u> soaked into the ground. Kenney said she also noticed Frazee's mother step briefly onto the porch, then return into the house.

Once the flames had simmered down [it's not clear whether the pair put the fire out,[80] and shovelled out the ashes where the tote once was, there and then, or if Frazee did it later], Kenney drove Frazee back

---

80 The fire didn't simmer down on the night of November 24th. This fact was established on Trial Day 5, when Kenney confirmed that the fire burned right through the night, and into the morning, as part of Frazee's effort to reduce Kelsey's flesh, bones and teeth to ashes and dust.

to the Conoco, parking out of sight at around 21:40. Before getting into his truck he gave her final, urgent instructions.

"We need to make it look like she's disappeared, not dead; you've got to help me do this. Get her phone as far from here as possible, then text her boss. It's this number…this number right here. Tell him she's going to visit her sick grandmother and won't be at work."

Curls of warm fog escaped the rancher's mouth in the night air as Frazee advised Kenney. Whenever Kenney responded, a puff of fog erupted from her lips, an echo of the smoke and fire they had played at together, earlier in what had become a very long day. Kenney was also instructed to text Frazee from Kelsey's phone:

"Do you even love me?"

Kenney likely took grim, if ironic satisfaction from fake sending that text. Kenney said she also had Kelsey's purse and gun.

The twelve hour drive back to Idaho appeared to take place just as the drive down had, after dark and through the night. Frazee ordered Kenney to text him photos from Kelsey's phone. Kenney didn't like that idea. She was nervous leaving a pinging digital trail going the way she was going. Kenney eventually turned off Kelsey's phone once she reached <u>Grand Junction, and as far as Salt Lake City, Utah</u>, where she turned it on again.

When Frazee called Kenney on Kelsey's phone, she was unnerved, and hastily pressed the power button, turning the device off.

After more than eleven hours behind the wheel, not far from Mad Gorge State Park, in Idaho, Kenney reactivated the device, texted Frazee:

"Do you even love me?"

And then texted Kelsey's boss. This second text would have been sent very early on Sunday morning, when Kenney was 45 minutes away from her own home. Then Kenney deactivated the device. She drove another five miles then called Frazee. Her message was dutiful, tired and terse.

"It's done."

Cover-Up

By mid-morning on November 25th – a Sunday – Kenney was back home. But she wasn't quite done. She burned Kelsey's phone[81] and purse in the back yard of her home in Kimberly, Idaho. She put the ashes of this incineration into a silver box, placed the box into a plastic bag and then disposed of the bag and box in a trash bin *en route* to work [presumably Monday morning]. She handed the gun to an unnamed friend, telling the friend it belonged to a crazy aunt.

On November 26th, a Tuesday, and just four days after Kelsey's murder, Frazee still had a lot on his mind. According to Kenney, the two were as thick as thieves, talking a lot. Kenney testified that it felt like Frazee was "coaching" her, instructing her on what to do, what to say but above all:

"Keep your mouth shut. If the cops call you, stick with the horse story."

Was this the romantic aftermath that she'd expected? Now that Kelsey was gone, things were worse than ever. She was starting to feel like a disposable commodity herself, only good to be told to do this, or told to do that.

---

81 It's not completely clear if Kenney burned the phone with the purse, or at separate time on December 5th, after the police seized Frazee's phone.

On December 2nd, the same day the Berreths finally became worried, Frazee contacted Kenney saying Cheryl had called him and wanted him to check on Kelsey. Frazee was also irritated by news reports saying Kelsey's phone had pinged near Gooding, Idaho.

Oh, God!

Frazee told Kenney to *stay cool.*

But things weren't cooling down, they were heating up fast. On December 3rd, the same day the Berreths arrived in Woodland Park, Frazee wasn't off feeding his cows. Instead, <u>he had gone into town to hire an attorney</u>. He instructed the attorney on his version of events, and further, empowered the attorney to "handle" the press with a version of events, which he'd signed off on. Kelsey wanted space, and wanted him – Frazee – to have custody of Kaylee[82] while she sorted her shit out.

Ironically, when Frazee – carrying Kaylee – made his way from the attorney's office to the parking lot where his pick-up was parked, an *ABC* news reporter intercepted him. Frazee ignored the reporter, but when he was cornered as he was exiting and locking the gate to his ranch by the very same *ABC* reporter, Frazee was, shall we say, <u>*less sanguine*</u>. [83]

If Frazee wasn't talking to the cops, or to the media, he couldn't stop talking to Kenney. He was calling her multiple times each day, until December 4th.[84] On that day the FBI seized Frazee's phone in a

---

82 The story of Kelsey wanting space was the same story Frazee told Kelsey's mother.

83 Speaking in a hoarse voice, Frazee turned on the reporter, snarled and pointed, while saying: <u>*"This is private property. This is a private road."*</u>

84 Frazee was arrested on December 21st, three long weeks after his last com-

parking lot in Colorado Springs. On December 5th he was questioned in connection with Kelsey's disappearance. That same day Frazee contacted an unnamed family member of Kenney's[85] and conveyed the message about destroying the evidence. Kenney claimed it was the day after this call, via a third party, that Kenney burned Kelsey's phone.

Kenney and Frazee both knew what to do at this point.

Stay cool.

Stay quiet.

Meanwhile, the media narrative was gaining steam. Awareness of Kelsey's disappearance was spreading like wildfire. People were saying things like, "This is the Watts case all over again." Journalists, behind closed doors, <u>were whispering exactly the same thing</u>.

Around ten days later Kenney attended a rodeo in Las Vegas. Just when the past seemed to be receding behind her an agent from the FBI contacted her. Kenney said she wasn't surprised by this call, as her ex-husband had called the night prior [December 13th], to say agents had come prowling, and asking for her. It's not clear whether this led to Kenney skipping town for Vegas, or whether she just happened to be in Vegas. Probably Kenney wanted to make herself scarce just in case.

Kenney let Chad know she thought she was being framed. She let him know her reasons for being in Florissant were perfectly normal, she'd gone horse shopping with Frazee on his ranch, that's all.

If we consider the psychology of this fake alibi, it corresponds broadly to the animalistic desire to replace one thoroughbred with another, for economic reasons, say. In a real sense, Kenney had to assume that Frazee was getting rid of one horse, so he could ride

---

munication with Kenney on December 4th.

85 Possibly Chad Lee, Kenney's ex-husband.

another. And we know he'd previously used the mindfuckery of this analogy with her when he asked her to choose between marrying Chad and him [and the mindfuckery worked].

"You can't ride two horses at the same time, so you need to make a choice."

Kenney admitted she lied to the agent, claiming she was scared if she didn't tow the line with Frazee, something might happen to her child. In effect, Kenney had bailed on her boyfriend the first moment law enforcement spoke to her. Kenney knew which side her bread was buttered on, and Frazee's game was over. So she switched sides. When she testified she claimed she knew "it was coming" [meaning, an accounting for the crime and her participation in it]. She added that she didn't feel comfortable, and further:

"I didn't know how to handle the situation."

On the other hand, one could argue that she did. She did a pretty good job *handling the situation* with Frazee, and when she found herself in a bind, she was pretty quick on the horse *handling that situation* too, wasn't she?

Having said that, if Kenney lied [and she did] she started off as a pretty unconvincing liar. For example, she quickly put her foot in it saying that a) she didn't know who Kelsey was and b) that she'd last seen Frazee six weeks earlier [as opposed to about half that time]. There was also a bunch of calls between the pair around the time of the incident that didn't reflect well on either of them.

When we see Kenney taking the cops through the various crimes scenes on December 21st [by then the game was well and truly up], Kenney appears to be falling apart. She's sniffing, and her face jerking. She seems to be struggling – and failing – to hold it together.

After about two days in Vegas Kenney returned home.[86] Well, the FBI and CBI were waiting for her. They were at her door, armed with a search warrant for buccal swabs. If that scenario wasn't calculated to scare the bejesus out of her, what would have? In any event it worked. But unlike Chris Watts, Kenney was wise in terms of *handling* law enforcement. She agreed to cooperate but said she wanted her attorney to assist her. Her attorney won her an incredibly sweet deal.

Three days later [December 20th] Kenney sat down with investigators to make a statement. The next day [December 21st] she walked the FBI step by step through every detail of her – and her dreamboat's – involvement in Kelsey Berreth's murder, including Kelsey's last words to Frazee as the blows rained down on her.

"Please stop..."[87]

---

86 Kenney returned home from Vegas on approximately December 17th. Within four days of her return, Frazee was arrested and charged with murder.

87 These words, without fail, made local, national and international headlines overnight at the end of Trial Day 4.

Cowboys, Burning Bodies and a Little Girl Listening

"Keep a little fire burning; however small, however hidden." — Cormac McCarthy, The Road

If America – and <u>the rest of the world</u> – wasn't <u>paying attention</u> to the first few days of the Frazee trial, <u>they were now</u>. <u>Sensational headlines</u> reverberated <u>through the ether</u> and across the airwaves. Overnight, the earth itself seemed to contract at the news. Drizzle fell in the darkness, as if <u>the sky above Colorado wept</u>. By the next morning, black ice gnawed at the nation's bridges and overpasses, as if some Higher Power had authorized the cold snap,[88] wanted everyone to stay home, to pause, to reflect, and yes, to mourn Kelsey's violent passing.

Between midnight and 02:00 in Teller County, freezing drizzle began to fall. It wasn't cold enough for the streets to freeze. Although Thursday morning would start out icy underfoot, with bruised grey

---

88 October 2019, coinciding with the start of the Frazee murder trial, was <u>Denver's fourth coldest October</u> in recorded weather history, and the fourth coldest start to a year in more than a decade. These cold climate records in Colorado persisted into November as well, particularly in Pueblo, Colorado Springs and Grand Junction.

skies swirling above, this would soon clear as the mercury lifted to a high of 52 degrees Fahrenheit.

It wasn't only the weather and the environment that seemed to darken a shade ahead of Trial Day 5. Both the star witness herself – Kenney – and the defendant – Frazee – delayed proceedings on Thursday morning. Both said they were feeling sick, or otherwise under the weather. Frazee, dressed in a buttoned-down shirt and khakis, was given medicine, and by 10:30, <u>Kenney had pulled herself together</u> sufficiently <u>to continue</u> where <u>she'd left off</u>. [89]

Before Kenney resumed, Judge Scott Sells addressed the court. Sells was back on the warpath on Thursday, about privacy and decorum in his court room. It had come to his attention that members of the public were surreptitiously recording portions of the trial [in relation to Kenney's testimony, no doubt, and perhaps it was her concerns that lead to the delay and her being "unwell"]. As a result, the Judge modified his original order. The public were required to turn off their phones completely, and warned of "severe consequences" if they didn't. The media protocols remained unaffected. Some journalists were actively typing the trial narrative into their devices in real time, and then emailing these to themselves for editing and fleshing out later.

The lead prosecutor stood up and asked Kenney to back up to the day the FBI and CBI intercepted Kenney at her home, the moment she returned from Vegas, on December 17th.

Next Viehman exhibited crime scene photos and footage. What Viehman wanted to do now was anchor the pertinent facts of Kenney's

---

89 Press photographers captured Kenney arriving at court through a back entrance. Kenney, dressed in a white sweater and black skirt appeared di-shevelled with her two-tone hair [blonde and dark] <u>hanging untidily over her shoulders.</u>

story with objective evidence. She started with the six bags of bloodied trash cleaned up at the townhome. What did Kenney do with all these trash bags? Well, she placed them on the left side of Kelsey's car. This was the exact spot where the cadaver dog alerted on December 6th, information Kenney had no way of knowing.

Next Kenney was shown photos of herself walking through the crime scene, pointing. Many on Twitter were confused by this, assuming it was a typo or miscommunication. Wasn't it Kenney in court, being shown photos of the crime scene, and pointing out various aspects in the photos? No, it was Kenney shown photos of herself at the crime scene, and explaining to the court what she was saying to investigators while she was *in situ* at the crime scene.

Kenney had to explain to the court why she, <u>dressed in dark POLICE CBI AGENT</u> branded garb, <u>including a CBI branded cap</u>, had to climb up to <u>a particular blood stain "up high"</u>, almost reaching the ceiling. She indicated <u>where she recovered a tooth fragment</u> in a pool of dried blood. She explained, referring to photos and footage, <u>how she moved the couch</u>, <u>wiped blood off the couch</u>, and wiped blood that had dripped behind the couch[90] and behind the wall. Kenney confirmed and repeated what she was describing on bodycam footage, and repeating what was recorded at the crime scene, thus making her sworn statements officially part of her sworn testimony in court [in other words, making it official in a fundamentally legal setting]. Frazee, meanwhile, scribbled furiously on a pad of paper in front of him.

Viehman wanted to know where Kelsey was, and where Kaylee was, when Frazee murdered Kelsey. Kenney said she believed <u>the crime had taken place downstairs</u>, in <u>the lounge</u>. Kenney revealed that <u>Kaylee</u>

---

90 Kenney confirmed that the wipe mark residues were from bleach and Windex.

was in a back room, in her jumper, when Frazee struck Kelsey the first time with a baseball bat. It's unclear whether the door to that ground floor back room was open or closed. When Kenney was shown photos of Kaylee in the jumper, Kenney wept.

Next Viehman introduced bodycam footage from a visit to the Frazee Ranch that same day, at about 08:30. CBI Agent Gregg Slater and a small team surrounded and chaperoned Kenney – now sporting extravagant black glasses – as she moved across the sun-drenched crime scene on the ranch, pointing out additional totes, and clarifying where, when and how the burn unfolded, as well as Frazee's and her respective roles in the incineration of Kelsey's remains. As Kenney spoke in the footage, the Kenney in court stared down in shame, whereas Frazee leaned forward, watching intently.

In the footage it became apparent just how many items Kenney threw into the fire on November 24th: bloodied curtains, towels, pillows, stuffed animals, cleaning supplies, all the clothing Kenney'd been wearing,[91] the pair of black tennis shoes she wore while cleaning the scene.

As Kenney described Frazee starting the fire inside a curved aluminium drinking drum without a bottom, Frazee's defense lawyer stood up to report a person drawing a sketch inside the courtroom. The Judge directed court deputies to seize the sketch pad, and tear out the sketches. The man was warned if he repeated the offence he could be

---

91 Kenney said she wore a white painter's suit when she cleaned up the crime scene on November 24th, along with a grey sweater underneath and black leggings. All of these items, as well as socks, shoes, shoe covers, her underwear, bra and hairnet were placed in trash bags and added to the fire. Additional items added to the fire included a large, white stuffed horse, wooden building blocks and plastic cookie cutters.

sentenced to six months in jail for contempt. The man was permitted to remain in court, and although proceedings resumed, more deputies were summoned to keep a careful watch on what the public were doing in the gallery, while this sensitive testimony was being heard.

Kenney described Frazee placing lengths of green tin over the fire to try to moderate the size of the enormous flames. Then, in the video, Slater could be heard referring to Frazee's mother Sheila, who'd come out onto the deck of the house to look at the fire according to Kenney. The reporters didn't comment on either Sheila's response to this comment, nor Frazee's.

Next prosecutors admitted a black XXL "Commander" tote with double metal clasps into evidence. Kenney confirmed it was <u>a visual match</u> for the one she saw with Kelsey's body inside. Then a cardboard box containing a gas can was entered as an exhibit. The gas can was shown to Kenney. Unexpectedly, the sight of the faded red-white can in court reduced Kenney once again to tears. Dabbing her eyes with a white tissue, Kenney confirmed it was the one used to fuel the fire.

After a recess and the lunch break, Kenney reviewed additional aspects of her testimony. She recalled that she could actually see Frazee's house from the burn site, and had seen his mother appear on the deck once the fire was actively burning. According to Kenney, Sheila Frazee appeared after her son attempted to mitigate the height of the searing furnace. Kenney said she couldn't be certain if Sheila saw her.[92]

---

92 If Kenney didn't know whether Sheila saw her, she clearly saw the fire. *KOAA* notes in this respect:
*While Frazee was starting the fire, Kenney said [Frazee's] mother…**came outside and looked at the fire from the deck.** [Kenney] said **Sheila came a little ways to look.***

During this review Kenney admitted the obvious – that she looked "briefly" at the tote ["just once"] and saw a *burning heap* and *rubble*. This single glimpse of a nondescript mound was what Kelsey – a 29-year-old single mother – had been reduced to. Kenney also provided more detail on statements Frazee had made to her about Kelsey. He'd told her he'd used Kelsey *for what she was worth*. This, Kenney said, referred to her utility to run errands such as watering his horses and similar duties. Obviously once they were in the midst of a custody battle, Kelsey would cease to be useful, and instead would be the opposite – a burden and a threat. A financial drain. And so, just like a ranch animal that went from being useful to of no use, how did one deal with that…?

In a most peculiar and most ironic moment, Kenney said she'd convinced Frazee that she too could perform these utilitarian tasks for him. And Frazee had responded with praise, saying:

"I know you can at least clean…"

Because Kenney had cleaned for him in the past.

The prosecution's star witness concluded her testimony on both a sympathetic and accusatory note. Sympathetic in terms of telling the court *"it was really hard for Frazee"*[93] managing the fire through the night, and into the next morning. When the fire had done its work, Frazee said he was going to dispose of the ash in a nearby creek, or at a

---

93 When 18-year-old ranch hand Kyle Ritchie testified on Trial Day 5 [after the defense cross-examined Kenney, Ritchie sketched a different portrait of Frazee's feeling about the furnace he'd made. Ritchie said Frazee described the fire as "decently big" and his impression of Frazee in the aftermath felt like "just another day at work." Ritchie said Frazee told him he'd burned deer and elk antlers inside the trough. Ritchie told Frazee he was bummed out about this, because he wanted the antlers.

garbage dump.[94] He would use two young ranch hands to clear up the site, but, Kenney pointed out, that didn't mean they knew what they were involved in.

Accusatory in terms of answering the prosecution when Viehman asked Kenney to point out the man who'd told her he'd beaten Kelsey to death with a baseball bat. Viehman asked Kenney if *that man* was present in court. Kenney simply answered, "Yes," and pointed. Frazee stared blankly in front of him, not registering the gesture nor reacting to it. He was doing his best to pretend that *that man* wasn't present in court.

---

94 It remains a mystery where Frazee disposed of Kelsey's ashes. Although dump sites were extensively searched, no signs of Kelsey's remains were found. It may be that Frazee didn't dispose of Kelsey's remains at either of the locations [river or dump] he claimed to Kenney. According to Ritchie, the waste from the fire was loaded into a cattle trailer and taken to <u>Teller County Waste</u> <u>depot</u>. On the same day, during the same trip to Teller County Waste, another ranch hand Samuel Dygert said Frazee drove to Colorado Springs and visited a scrap metal place. On this same errand Frazee apparently met up with his brother at a gas station.

Dad, CCTV Logs, Cadaver Dogs and a Tooth

"I figured out a way to kill her." — Patrick Frazee, according to Krystal Kenney

Overnight the headlines ringing out across America's media landscape focused on the little girl who witnessed – or must have overheard – her mother's murder from a neighboring room. Not all the headlines did. *The Denver Post* dealt instead, and at some length, with Frazee's defense attorney's attempts to discredit Kenney during a lengthy cross-examination. *The Denver Channel* highlighted another counter by defense counsel: why Kenney never alerted anyone to Frazee's ongoing murder plot.

Adam Steigerwald's cross-examination on Trial Day 5 was at times scathing. According to *The Gazette* Steigerwald told Kenney:

"You drove 750 miles with a baseball bat. The purpose of that baseball bat was to kill Kelsey Berreth."

"It was at Patrick's request," Kenney responded.

"No baseball bats in Teller County?" Steigerwald fired back.

It's a damning indictment for sure, driving in a particular direction, towards someone who ultimately was a victim of murder, with a murder weapon, while claiming throughout to be in two minds about it. Clearly if Kenney was in two minds, more of her mind was sold on the scheme than wasn't. The remainder of the cross-examination is dealt with in the *Bittersweet* chapter in the final section.

#9 SIDNEY[95]

Krystal Kenney's father indicated his daughter had been living with him, on and off, throughout much of 2019 as her fortunes fluctuated from mysterious mistress to despised pariah. Sidney said despite her recent misfortune, he and his daughter remained close.

According to Kenney's father, she was a happy child, easy to please and good at whatever she decided to do. Kenney's father characterized his daughter as a people pleaser:

"She likes people and she likes people to like her."[96]

Next, prosecutor Beth Reed asked Sidney about the Kenney family's plans for Thanksgiving. Sidney told the court the plan was for the whole Kenney clan to sit down together for dinner that afternoon. Both Kenney and her ex-husband Chad were present at Sidney's house. Curiously, when Kenney was off [in terms of living on and off with her father] she was on with her ex-husband, continuing to live with him despite being officially divorced. At around 18:30 Kenney left the family gathering, although Sidney noted she disappeared for an hour to help Chad herd up a few cows that had escaped from their enclosure.

Kenney never said anything about driving to Colorado that weekend. The next time Sidney saw his daughter, he told the court, was around 19:00 on the 23rd. Once again, Kenney didn't say anything to

---

95 Sidney Kenney was the prosecution's 29th witness.

96 Source: *The Denver Channel*

her father about her intentions. Sidney said the next time he saw her was late on November 25th, or 26th, he couldn't be sure.

Sidney didn't have much knowledge on Frazee. Kenney's father remembered his name coming up around eight to ten years prior. He told the court he didn't have a positive impression of the rancher from Florissant.

The defense had little to cross Sidney on besides the fact that he confirmed Kenney's mother lived in Colorado, so it wasn't unusual for her to go to Colorado to see her.

#10 ADAMS [RECALLED TO THE STAND]

After Sidney Kenney, the prosecution sought to put both the mistress and the murderer at the scene, or within the apposite timeline, by calling up independent witnesses. The first was Shannon Kadiuraus, a Sonic employee. Kadiuraus was general manager at the Woodland Park branch in November 2018. It was Kadiuraus who was approached by Woodland Park Police Commander Chris Adams on December 20th [and the same day Kenney made her statement], with a request to pull the surveillance video logs from November 24th. Incredibly, despite the span of a few weeks, Kadiuraus was able to search for footage of Kenney in the borrowed black Passat, retrieve them and hand them over.

Next, prosecutor Beth Reed called up William David Stover. Stover was the IT manager responsible for the CCTV files at the Conoco gas station situated at 2636 W. Highway 24 in Florissant, a stone's throw from the Frazee Ranch. Presumably when Commander Adams contacted Kadiuraus at Sonic on December 20th, he also contacted Stover for the Conoco video footage. Stover didn't do much on the stand besides identify himself, confirm he was in charge of the particular gas station's

CCTV data, and testify that yes, Commander Adams had asked him to hand over the applicable files if he had them – and he did.

Now prosecutor Beth Reed called the investigating officer to the stand. It was the second time Commander Adams had been called to testify. On this go-round the state wanted Adams to lead the jury by the hand through the CCTV footage. Him – not the respective employees at Sonic or Conoco.

Not surprisingly, at the Conoco in Florissant there was a lot more footage not only of Kenney, but Frazee as well. Why? Well, because the pair used this nondescript little gas station [just 4 minutes' drive and 1.4 miles from the burn site] as their base of operations to swap vehicles, buy burning fuel for their homemade volcano and ultimately, chose the station for exchange instructions about Kelsey's phone. The station was also the point where they bid farewell to one another when Kenney finally headed back to Idaho late that Saturday night.

The CCTV narrative from the Conoco cameras makes for interesting reading:[97]

<u>**November 24th, Saturday Afternoon and Evening [Day 2 of Kelsey's Disappearance]**</u>

16:17: *Black Volkswagen Passat enters Conoco parking lot. Drives beyond the range of the surveillance cameras to a rear or peripheral parking area.*

16:32: *Frazee arrives 15 minutes later in his red pickup. He's well-dressed in jeans, a mustard-colored sweatshirt, a sleeveless khaki fleece, and khaki cap. Frazee is wearing gloves and has the hood of his sweatshirt pulled over his cap.*

---

97 Source: *The Denver Channel*

16:35: *Frazee fills his truck with gas, then enters the Conoco. When he emerges* <u>*he starts filling up a sun-bleached red-white gas can [six gallons]*</u>*. Once done,* <u>*at about 16:37 Frazee hoists the gas can into the bed of his truck.*</u>

16:39: *Frazee drives off the gas pump apron to a peripheral parking area.* <u>*The black tote is no longer visible in the back of the truck.*</u> *Adams speculates that Frazee parked alongside Kenney's car to discuss what they were going to do next. They agreed to leave the Passat in the parking area, and drive together to start the fire by the kennels.*

16:48: *After nine minutes of discussion, Frazee and Kenney left for the Nash Ranch together in his truck. Frazee drove. Kenney sat beside him in the passenger seat. Why did they spend nine minutes talking in the cold, in the Conoco's desolate parking lot? Frazee probably wanted to examine the six garbage bags to make sure Kenney had cleaned up after all, and to factor the bags into his pyrotechnics.*

18:57: *Two hours and nine minutes later, Frazee's red pickup pulls into the Conoco again, this time heading straight to the parking area and Kenney's vehicle.*[98] *According to Kenney's testimony she returned alone in the red pickup to the borrowed Passat to retrieve the six trash bags. She then transferred the trash bags to Frazee's truck, and drove to the Frazee Ranch.*[99]

18:59: *Two minutes later the red pickup leaves the area, and heads east on Highway 24.*

---

98 It's not clear whether the black tote was visible at this time.

99 This is possibly an error. *The Denver Channel* reports Kenney drove her Passat to the Nash Ranch at this time, and returned in the same vehicle with Frazee and the black tote. However it seems unlikely that they would only start the fire after 21:37.

21:37: *The red pickup*[100] *returns to the Conoco parking lot. According to Kenney, both Kenney and Frazee are inside the car. They return to retrieve Kenney's vehicle.*

21:40: *The black Passat leaves the Conoco area for the last time, turning west on the highway and heading down the route toward Salt Lake City and Idaho. The red pickup exits seconds later, turning the opposite direction, towards the fire still burning fiercely on his ranch.*

Adams concludes his testimony by revealing how investigators even discovered a receipt timestamped approximately16:30[101] for $75 in gasoline from Frazee's home corresponding to the time CCTV footage puts him at the Conoco. [102]

Now let's deal with the K9 units.

#11 HURST [RADAR][103]

If Trial Day 5 was grisly and gruelling, this part of Trial Day 6 was too. Incredibly, seven different canines were employed in the search for Kelsey on Frazee's property on December 14th. Not one alerted anywhere, at any time, including at the burn site, which shows how effective flames and fuel are at defeating the foil of cadaver traces.

In February 2018, Mike Hurst, a K9 handler from the Elizabeth Police Department, was called to do a scent check at the Nash Ranch. [104] Hurst led his hefty cadaver dog Radar, a 140-pound bloodhound,

---

100 *The Denver Channel* describes the black Passat leaving at 18:59 and returning to the parking lot at 21:37. This is possibly an error.

101 Frazee arrived two minutes earlier than the time on the receipt – if the Conoco's CCTV clock is accurate.

102 Investigators also discovered three wooden baseball bats in Frazee's home.

103 K9 Handler Mike Hurst was the prosecution's 26th witness.

104 Julie Nash testified on Trial Day 6 about leasing grazing rights to the Nash

on a search through the red barn on Nash Ranch, as well as the tractor parked inside.

Despite the passage of almost three months, <u>Radar alerted traces of human decomposition on the top of a pile of 12-foot high hay bales</u>. [105] Next the prosecution presented a photo from December 21st [when Kenney did her walk-through of the various crime scenes] depicting <u>discolorations and indentations on the top of one bale</u>. <u>The indentations also appeared damp or wet</u>.

#12 EBERLE [LUCY][106]

Brian Eberle's cadaver dog Lucy, also a bloodhound, was requested to scent the scene at Woodland Park fairly early in the game – December 4th. Eberle was asked to have Lucy "run around the vehicles" in Kelsey's driveway.

There were no indications on Kelsey's Chevy truck [registered to her parents], but once Lucy sniffed around Kelsey's Toyota, Lucy alerted to human remains on the rear corner of the sedan on the driver's side. It's pretty amazing that despite ten days of exposure to all sorts of weather – wind, sun, snow and cold – the canine alerted [by laying down beside the scent source] at the exact spot Kenney identified *in situ* seventeen days later as the spot where she'd placed the six garbage bags.

Ranch to Frazee. These rights included the use of the barn. Nash said he was also provided with a key to the property in November 2018. According to Nash no one besides Frazee had access to the property; he was the sole lessor at the time. Nash also confirmed in court that Frazee stored hay and his tractor on the property and in the barn.

105 Radar's alert, based on the video, doesn't seem "strong" or convincing.

106 K9 Handler Brian Eberle was the prosecution's 27th witness.

There was also a second indication from Lucy – in the upstairs bathroom on Kelsey's underwear. This is impressive in itself. It shows despite Kenney's Herculean efforts during her four hour cleaning marathon, Lucy had sniffed her way to critical, game changing evidence that proved Kelsey was no longer alive.

Before Eberle was dismissed, Judge Sells had a few questions of his own. He wanted to know whether cadaver dogs are trained to scent with bleach and other pungent chemicals present. Eberle said they weren't, because these chemicals could damage the canine's olfactory senses, just as loud music can damage the ears.

#12 PETERSON[107]

FBI Agent Donald Peterson, a crime scene analyst, was the team leader on the December 21st search of the Frazee Ranch.[108] A single, vital piece of evidence had somehow survived the inferno. It was still there, lying in the dirt despite a number of scent searches by dogs, and several searches by the FBI, CBI and law enforcement.

According to *KRDO's* report on this aspect of the trial:

*In the afternoon of Trial Day 6, FBI agents testified about what they found at the burn spot on Frazee's property in Florissant. In previous searches in mid-December, they said they didn't find any biological or decomposition evidence in their excavations. **[But] when [Kenney] pointed out the burn spot, investigators [discovered] an inch of topsoil***

---

107 FBI Special Agent Donald Peterson, based in Denver, was the prosecution's 36th witness. A total of five FBI agents testified one after the other regarding evidence found at the burn site. Besides Peterson, these agents included Charles DeFrance, Ashley Cape, Janie Rojhani and Stephanie Benitiz.

108 FBI Agent Donald Peterson was also part of the Frazee Ranch searches on December 14th and 15th, as well as Kelsey's townhome on December 19th. Peterson participated in four *in situ* searches *in toto*.

and gravel that had been poured recently [to cover and conceal the burn site]. The investigators said it was hard to notice unless you were looking right at it. When [investigators] removed the top layer, they found a crust of plastic coating underneath, according to testimony. Next to the crust was a soiled spot that was wet with oil and other debris.

On the stand, FBI Agent Peterson directed the court's attention to the burn area using crime scene photos. Peterson indicated <u>a discoloured patch on the surface of the driveway</u> with an irregular black stain in the foreground, and a lighter, damper, more consistently-shaped rounded brown frame on the upper and left fringe of the black stain. In parts the black and brown stain were mixed together, but the very top of the stain was *only-brown* while the very bottom was *only-black*. The only-brown stain was consistent with liquid. The irregular only-black stain was consistent with melted plastic.

Peterson also pointed out that the deck of the Frazee Ranch home was visible from the burn site. Incredibly, Frazee had chosen a site in plain sight – the road surface – to build his inferno. With the dogs nearby, anyone who came sniffing in the area would lead to the dogs barking and alert the residents of the house. In this way Frazee felt he could maintain a vigil over Kelsey's remains, or rather, the remains of her funeral pyre. And each day a vehicle or feet traffic moved over the stain, it would be absorbed into the fabric of the ranch itself.

But Frazee hadn't counted on Kenney blabbing about everything to the cops. The question was, having pointed out the stain, would investigators be able to unearth anything *tangible*? It was there, tiny, glinting, in the dust, but would the investigators have the patience and sensitivity to find it?

Peterson gave the horizontal dimensions of the burn area as eight feet by five feet. It may not seem like much. Like looking for a golf ball on thirteen football fields where the grass has been allowed to grow to more than twice its usual length. It's not so much difficult work as tedious. Working systematically, section by section, field by field, making sure each area is meticulously and systematically checked before moving on to the next block.

Next, Peterson took the jury through the tools, equipment,[109] protocols and procedures used to analyze the burn site. He said once they'd removed the gravel "carpet", he immediately smelled burned plastic. A team of four warmly-dressed excavators, including Peterson, worked on the scalded burn surface using a small pickaxe and brushes. The first step was to gently expose the full extent of the burn area, as well as to delineate a crime scene perimeter in the dirt.

Once the surface layer of gravel had been brushed and dusted away, a plastic crust was revealed. The plastic had fused into the substrate. Although the melt stain appeared mostly smooth and flat in the vertical plane [indicative of previous scraping efforts, and perhaps flattening and levelling], in the horizontal plane it was irregular. It was possible tiny fragments of evidence may have resisted efforts at removal within these irregularities.

The large, damp stain, as well as the slanted surface of the substrate, meant tiny pieces of evidence may have floated on or flowed out of the central furnace area downhill[110] on a liquid, or fluid mixture of

---

109 At least two large green and yellow shovels can be seen lying on the ground, in the dirt, behind Peterson's team of crime scene excavators at the burn site.

110 Peterson was explicit in indicating that the "wet spot" was on the down-hill side of the burn patch. This is indicative that gravity drew the fluid out of the central pyre, as the tote slowly melted down.

some kind, thereby also removing these tiny traces from the core area targeted by the ranch hands during their initial clean up.

On the bottom rim of the black stain, Peterson noted, along the margin where the crust ended and the stain began, <u>the melted plastic was slightly raised, and curved.</u> Peterson suggested that something shaped like an arc [the bottom edge of the water trough] may have allowed the melted plastic to build-up here, while also preventing it from draining further downhill. Meanwhile, fluids that were less thick than the plastic, found a way through or under openings in the trough.

The excavators chipped through, and chipped up all the pieces of melted plastic. They sifted through other small materials in the burnt pit area – pebbles, tiny pieces of wire,[111] nondescript fragments that may have been vegetation or slivers of sackcloth, or clothing. Ordinary dirt was collected and put through a sieve.

After hours on site, sitting on the cold, hard, acrid-smelling, slanted substrate, sifting, dusting, scoping and scraping, the team inspected a final section of dirt. It was time to call it a day to the careful search. They'd done their best.

Back to _KRDO's_ report:

According to testimony, it was on the last shovel of dirt that an agent found what [was] believed to be a tooth. It turned out to be a partial tooth…

---

111 Kyle Ritchie, one of the ranch hands said he used a magnet on the burn site to pick up hundreds of nail fragments – from the pallets – to prevent them from causing punctures to wheels operating on the drive. These sharp nails remained behind after the parent wood was turned to ash.

When the tooth was analyzed it was found to be female, and human.[112] But there wasn't enough DNA on it to conclusively match it to Kelsey.

---

112 Diane France, a forensic anthropologist, and the 65th [in other words one of the last] prosecution witness, testified that the fragment was human and female. France's testimony is discussed in more detail in *MURDER MOST FOUL MISTRESS ON TRIAL*, the second book in the No Body No Crime Book series.

Moore's Law

"Moore's Law states that processing power for computers will double every two years."
— Wikipedia

What does Moore's Law – the computing term about processing power doubling every two years – have to do with Joseph Paul Moore, Frazee's long-time friend and the prosecution's 39th witness? Simply put, with time comes *complexity*, and with greater complexity, some things speed up. Does that include true crime, and if so, how so?

Let's have a look.

#13 MOORE[113]

After the lunch break on Trial Day 6 one of the most important witnesses, if not *the* most important witness in the eleven-day murder trial, took the stand. In 2001 or 2003 Moore, a rancher himself, recalled offering Frazee a job. He described Frazee as an excellent cattleman, and in footage that is out there, <u>Frazee can be seen roping steers</u> at what appears to be rodeo fairs.

---

113 Joseph Paul Moore was a close confidant of Patrick Frazee. He testified on Trial Day 6, and was the prosecution's 39th witness. Moore provides some of the deepest insight into the true identity of Frazee.

Before that, Moore recalled meeting Frazee for the first time when Frazee was a ten-year-old kid. Even then he knew Frazee as a cowboy; a rancher who rode horses, knew livestock and got his hands and cowboy boots dirty. Moore described a close relationship with the younger Frazee going back at least two decades. Moore seemed in some ways a mentor, and in others, a father-figure and confidant.

In 2018, Moore described his relationship with Frazee as good, observing also how Frazee had so many good things going for him. Evidently Frazee [like Chris Watts] didn't share Moore's opinion.

Moore's attachment to a man he sometimes referred to as his "step-kid" became clear when he teared up on the stand. According to _The Denver Channel_ Moore testified at one point:

"You just don't want [to] picture somebody that you've known this long and trusted – **you just don't want to think that they could do something like this."**

Moore and Frazee were so close, if Moore left town:

[Moore] would call Frazee and have him come check on his animals while they were gone.

It's through Moore that we're provided with a rare glimpse into the dynamic of Frazee's relationship with Kelsey. It's through the prism of the rancher, but it's also of vital importance that it is: because that's what Frazee was – through and through, balls to bone – a rancher.

According to _The Denver Channel_:

Moore said the first time he met [Kelsey] was at a ranch around November 2016, when [Kelsey] was helping move Frazee's calves. Moore said Berreth did not know how to handle all the cows, having never been in that situation before. He testified that **Frazee was not pleased with**

her. *"He berated her horribly," Moore said. "He yelled at her, cussed at her, just terribly."*

One wouldn't expect Moore to lie about this. After all, he's close with Frazee, or was. If anything, one might expect him to soften the reality of this experience. What this shows is not just Frazee's temperament, but his attitude to Kelsey in terms of his identity, his lifestyle and effectively, his livelihood. And what we see is *incompatibility*. The idea that Kelsey grew up on a farm may have appealed to Frazee in the beginning, but the reality was Kelsey's rural upbringing didn't really translate to cattle herding. Kenney's rodeo background – one imagines – was more compatible, and yet we know what Kenney thought after doing chores for Frazee, only to have him criticize her.

Kelsey probably didn't do anything wrong...

You just don't want to think that they could do something like this.

This may also explain, at least in part, why Kelsey didn't live on the ranch, but half an hour away. Since Kelsey had proved she wasn't of any use on the ranch, why should she live on the ranch? Another factor in this equation was likely Frazee's mother, and her feelings towards Kelsey. One imagines, since Frazee was effectively looking after her while his mother was providing him with square meals and lodging, Sheila was only too happy not to have someone else around competing for her son's attention, and affections.

Ominously, despite his close friendship with Frazee, Frazee seemed to keep the fact of Kelsey's pregnancy secret from Moore [something Watts also did, to some extent, with his colleagues]. Frazee claimed he didn't know about the pregnancy *until Kelsey was at the hospital giving birth.*

And it's at this point that things went haywire with Frazee. Whereas Chris Watts's behavior got weird when Shan'ann fell pregnant for the third time, Frazee started going off the rails after Kaylee's birth. Troublingly, Frazee's slurs in the beginning were directed not at Kelsey, but at his infant daughter.

*"….kids go missing all the time from playgrounds
and schoolyards…"*

Frazee seemed to have a very simple psychology in terms of his problems [again, similar to Watts]. If something was a problem, make the problem disappear. Get rid of it. If the something that was a problem was a person, why not make the person disappear?

"People go missing all the time. No body, no crime…"

Moore admitted that Frazee told him he was "having trouble with someone." Each time Frazee said something about kids or people going missing, Moore chided him, telling him not to say things like that. Frazee would invariably respond that he was only kidding, but if there's one thing truer in true crime than anywhere else it's Chaucer's aphorism:

<u>Many a true word is spoken in jest…</u>

Moore also described the ranchers joking amongst themselves. In one instance Frazee mentioned meeting a hit man for the mob. Moore brushed it off, believing a hit man would never identify himself. It's not clear whether Moore chuckled and laughed before brushing it off. Then, on April 26th, 2018 [Moore could recall the exact date, because it was the same day both ranchers ran their bulls over to a neighboring ranch] Frazee's loose talk escalated a notch. *The Denver Channel* cited Moore's testimony as follows:

Moore…asked Frazee how things were going with Kaylee Jo's mom [Moore's reference to Kelsey]. Frazee responded: 'I figured out a way to kill her.' And I went, 'Don't even talk about things like that. Get that shit out of your head.' He just kind of grinned and said, 'No body, no crime, right?'"

Moore told Frazee again:

"Get that shit out of your head."

But Frazee didn't. Frazee couldn't. If Frazee's original target was Kaylee, for reasons of efficacy, that target had now pendulumed to Kelsey. <u>The seed had already started germinating in his psychology.</u> It was growing, branching out into the thin, skeletal fingers of criminal psychology. As the psychology developed, so did the thing driving it.

<u>The Denver Channel</u> describes Frazee telling Moore about how he was stalking Kelsey, including having people spying on her and photographing her. [This is likely untrue, but part of Frazee's effort to discredit his former fiancé].

[He was] taking pictures of her because he said he wanted to sue her for custody of Kaylee. Moore said Frazee sounded serious about his claims. **Frazee claimed to have a picture from one of these people of [Kelsey's] car outside a liquor store.** *The car was running and Kaylee was inside, Frazee told Moore. Moore asked to see the photograph and Frazee said it was on his computer at home. Moore said he never asked about it again.*

This image likely never existed. It was Frazee's way of sketching a picture that put Kelsey in a bad light. If Kelsey was seen as dysfunctional and broken, her disappearance or death would make more sense. So Frazee worked at establishing this narrative. We see a mirror here in his criminal psychology: he places a bogus narrative not only following her disappearance, but inserts it in advance as well. <u>Frazee thought it was a brilliant plan</u>. This is why when Kelsey disappeared, those who knew Frazee, and some who knew Kelsey [or knew of her through Frazee], weren't surprised. Well they weren't surprised <u>because it was all part of the plan.</u>[114]

---

114 This chapter is an abbreviated version of Moore's testimony. The remainder is covered in the *INTERTEXUALITY* section of this book, as well as in the *Joking around with Moore's Law* chapter of *MURDER MOST FOUL MISTRESS ON TRIAL*, the second book in the No Body No Crime Book series.

Snitch

"I would really like to see Krystal with a bullet in her head. Piss and shit on her face. Fucking dirty cunt ass bitch." — Words attributed to Patrick Frazee by Jacob Bentley, a jailhouse snitch

On the final Friday of the trial the Teller County courtroom was a full house. A large contingent of media were present along with an estimated 30 public spectators. Many of these new visitors were in court in anticipation of Frazee taking the stand.

Inside the court, the newbies glanced curiously at the man at the center of the murder trial. He was seated on the left side of the courtroom neatly dressed in a blue-striped button-down shirt. Frazee, as usual, had a pen and notepad handy for scribbling notes.[115]

On Trial Day 10[116] everyone was surprised by a witness no one saw coming. Not even the prosecution did. In the *CBS* documentary *Justice for Kelsey Berreth*, prosecutor Beth Reed admits they didn't know about the snitch until *he* contacted them – wait for it – *during* the 10-day trial.

---

115 Frazee's handwritten notes in court were handy facsimiles for the notes Bentley would eventually introduce.

116 Trial Days 7, 8 and 9 are analyzed in-depth in *MURDER MOST FOUL MISTRESS ON TRIAL*, available in January 2020.

At approximately 39-minutes into the documentary, Reed acknowledges that the former inmate "started calling our office [the District Attorney's office]" while they were in court, leading their case. Reed admits in the documentary, smiling broadly:

"We didn't know about him…[referring to the snitch]."

If you the reader are still hesitant, or even cynical, about the relevance of applicability of Intertextuality in true crime, this aspect from the inmate, may correct that notion. In the *CBS* documentary where it deals with the snitch, the documentary refers to <u>another</u> *CBS* documentary which the snitch said he watched. This one: <u>*The Murder of Kelsey Berreth*</u> [released on October 9th,[117] only a month prior to Trial Day 10]. The inmate was fascinated by the coverage because Frazee had been his neighbor in jail. Not just that, Frazee had given the inmate – a gang member – a hit list handwritten on paper towels.

Frazee ordered the inmate to flush the towels after reading them, but instead Jacob Bentley[118] kept them and waited for an opportunity to use them as leverage. When the trial was in full swing, Bentley seized his chance.

---

117 CBS' <u>*Justice for Kelsey Berreth*</u> was released after the trial, and verdict, on November 24th, 2019.

118 Jacob Bentley was the prosecution's 75th and final witness. CBI Agent Gregg Slater was briefly recalled [for the second time] to corroborate Bentley's testimony and to authenticate the handwriting on the paper towels as authentic, belonging to Frazee. Counting Slater's three separate sessions on the stand, the prosecution called a total of 76 witnesses. When Judge Sells asked the defense whether they, or indeed Frazee, would call any witnesses, Frazee spoke four words, the most words he'd uttered during the three-week trial. Frazee said: "I will remain silent."

Before we deal with Bentley's testimony, and the contents of those paper towels, let's deal with another, equally disturbing witness: the blood spatter expert.

#14 PRIEST[119]

Jonathyn Priest's testimony reduced Kelsey's father Darrell – sitting in the front-row of the Teller County courtroom – to tears.[120] As those in the gallery sitting alongside Darrell Berreth handed him tissues, and patted his rocking shoulders, Priest sketched in vivid, visceral detail, how Kelsey's blood splattered and sprayed across the walls of her home as she was being bludgeoned to death.

On the final day of the prosecution's case, <u>footage</u> was presented <u>of Kenney holding up a broom</u> to show a spot <u>10-12 feet high</u> <u>where she'd cleaned Kelsey's blood</u>. The blood spatter expert maintained that these <u>extensive spray patterns</u> were consistent not only with Kenney's witness account, but also with a *high-impact attack* using a blunt object. Priest, while motioning with his hands and arms, illustrated the impact arcs that could be caused. Next Priest held up <u>a wooden sample taken from the floor of Kelsey's townhome</u>. He showed the court two clear indentations forcefully embedded into the wood of the plank. The expert couldn't definitively say what made these impressions, just that Frazee must have missed Kelsey at least twice during his rain of devastating blows.

But <u>Priest pointed out</u>:

"…something substantially heavy and substantially hard had an impact on this area and certainly a baseball bat is consistent with that…"

---

119 Jonathyn Priest was the prosecution's 74th [third-last] witness.

120 Source: *The Denver Post*

Priest also referred to <u>lengthy bloodstains found between the floor planks</u>. These had seeped between the planks from an extensive pool of blood that had collected on the floor surface of the lounge.

Through the testimony of the blood spatter expert, the white interior of Kelsey's home was suddenly reimagined scarlet with blood spatter. Tiny drops even coated kitchen appliances, kitchen chairs and the baby gate.

<u>Priest added</u>:

"The fact that there are small bloodstains supports my opinion that we have a forceful incident, not a passive one."

Priest concluded that the victim [he didn't refer to Kelsey by name] was struck repeatedly while she crouched on the floor in agony. Priest estimated she may have been struck ten to fifteen times. Bloody footprints found leaving this "ground zero" showed a person stepping in and out of a pool of blood while they walked around.

#15 BENTLEY

Just like Kenney, Frazee repeatedly approached Bentley, asking the inmate in 17 letters to murder a "hit list" – people who could sink his fortunes at trial. <u>At the top of that list</u> was none other than Krystal Kenney.

<u>On one paper towel Frazee wrote</u> [presumably referring to Kenney]:

I know from discovery and evidence that they were both in contact and that she herself tried hire a hit person/solicitation. I also know the DA has scripted her on details to give statements that match up with evidence. They helped put words in her mouth.

<u>In another note</u> Frazee wrote:

I'd [it'd] be nice if she disappeared and didn't show up for trial. Just turned one way and was never seen again. Any ideas?

The list also included <u>Kenney's ex-husband</u>, and suggestions <u>to "snag his phone and watch the kids"</u> as well as Kenney's best friend Michelle Stein, Frazee's neighbor and confidant Joe Moore, and Joe Moore's significant other Wendi Clarke.[121]

Under the list of names Frazee was adamant:

- *They <u>all</u> need to disappear unseen till at least November 22nd after the trial*

- *Wendi Clarke is the cash cow. Joe has all kinds of shit to sell*

<u>The Denver Channel</u> cited these notes, entered into evidence, by number. There were 17 in all, but the media was careful to leave out the more graphic, as well as those providing personal details such as telephone numbers and addresses:

Letter 1 read, "You know where to find Krystal Jean Lee Kenney? Chad Lee?..." The letter listed out who each individual is...[Bentley] wrote in letter 8 that the planning got his blood flowing. "If I walk out, you and me could pull of all kinds of shit. I know all kinds of rich ranchers around the west." In letter 9, Frazee referred to the DA's office working with Kenney...In letter 13, Frazee allegedly said "I'm not the monster they say I am. I don't know what happened or where she went."

As damning as all this was against Frazee, in none of his correspondence to the snitch did he admit to doing anything himself. Curiously, there's another intertextuality here, where Frazee, <u>just like</u>

---

121 Kelsey's mother <u>Cheryl was also identified as a "Side Idea"</u> on Frazee's hit list.

<u>Chris Watts</u>, appeared to be the most worried that others – even fellow criminals – might think of him as a monster.[122]

Back to *The Denver Channel*:

In letter 15, Frazee wrote: "I'm excited if we can pull this off, only thing better would be if Krystal sent someone a text from her home confessing and telling the truth that I didn't have anything with it to do at all. Slater and then all five disappear."

Perhaps the most sinister aspect in all seventeen notes was Frazee's reference to his mother Sheila. It appears to be the only cell phone number Frazee provided to his fellow-inmate, showing the extent to which he considered her an ally. Frazee then instructed Bentley:

Pass a message to her [Sheila] via text or call [but] use a <u>fake name</u>.

<u>Frazee then provided two apparently coded messages</u> he knew – or expected – his mother would understand. Frazee underlined both:

<u>*All the horses are taken care of*</u>

or

<u>*Have her tell me that the Elk hunt was successful*</u>

"Horses" and "elk" seemed to be a reference to people Frazee had on his hit list, doesn't it? If so, this corresponds to statements Frazee made as alibis to the cops, to Cheryl Berreth and for Kenney and him to both use, such as "feeding his cows" or "going to look at a horse" when he was really preoccupied with homicide. Frazee also told his ranch hands that he'd made a huge fire *to burn elk antlers* – once again using an animal as a proxy for Kelsey.

---

122 Bentley seemed to be convinced Frazee was a monster, which is why he held onto the paper towels and treated them like gold.

And just as Frazee had manipulated Kenney into helping him in order to "protect" his daughter, Frazee was at it again with Bentley, <u>signing off one of his longest notes with</u>:

Help! Help! ME PLEASE MAN!

I repay how Ever! ***My life and my little***

Girls life depends on You!

Throw me down your Plans/Ideas

When Bentley was asked why he'd come forward, <u>he answered</u> ironically, "Honestly…I was hoping to get some sort of help in my case…" He seemed to be suggesting he'd called the prosecutors' office for legal advice. In any event, he wanted other help as well from the prosecutors. Some sort of deal if he testified in court. And hey, the prosecutors had made a deal with the devil, so why not with him? According to <u>The Denver Post</u>:

Bentley said he told Frazee he was part of a prison gang and that Frazee offered to help bail him out of jail if he arranged the killings of Kenney and other witnesses…Bentley would be the last witness called in the trial.

Bentley's testimony anchored the prosecution's case. They ended strongly with a shocker, using Frazee's own words to damn him. It was arguably the most jaw-dropping testimony in a trial jam-packed with stunning revelations.

But Bentley's most damning note was withheld by almost all in the mainstream media covering the trial. One reporter, <u>Sam Kraemer</u>, recorded what he described as "probably the most graphic of the notes", substituting asterisks where expletives were used, and warning his audience that what they were about to read was disturbing.

"I would really like to see Krystal with a bullet in her head. Piss and shit on her face. Fucking dirty cunt ass bitch."

After the prosecution rested, Judge Sells asked defense counsel if they were going to call any witnesses. Frazee broke his silence, which he'd maintained throughout the three-week trial, uttering just four words:

"I will remain silent."

It wasn't necessary for Frazee to say anything. He'd said enough, and his actions, though sly and secretive, and despite all his schemes, had come back to haunt him.

TRUE CRIME INTERTEXTUALITIES – FRAZEE/WATTS

"No body, no crime – right?" — Patrick Frazee to Joseph Moore

Frazee's Chores on December 5 and 11 and the Chris Watts Case

"All you gotta do is hit her in the head and put her in the trash can." — Patrick Frazee, according to Kenney, and <u>repeated by Jennifer Viehman in her opening statement</u> on November 1st, 2019

One day after Patrick Frazee's arrest on December 21st, 2018, I posted <u>the True Crime Rocket Science assessment on Patrick Frazee</u> on *CrimeRocket.com*. In the title, and throughout the body text of the article I reinforced the notion of a link – a relationship – between the Frazee case and the Watts case.

The first words of the article summed it up quite nicely:

Time. That's the main difference between the Frazee case and Watts case.

I also provided ten similarities between the two cases, before concluding:

*The big question is **whether Frazee was aware of, and attempted to learn from the "mistakes" of the Watts case…**There is a very clear indicator for this being not merely possible, but probable. Can you see what it is?*

This "clear indicator" is the singular *idiosyncrasy* common to both the Frazee and Watts cases. That *idiosyncrasy* is the shared psychology of disposing of human remains in an attempt to completely destroy them.

Watts went to a lot of effort to transport the bodies in his custody and to dispose of them in a way we may alternatively describe as heinous and despicable, but also unusual. He meant to *dissolve the cadavers* of his children so that they would, eventually, disappear entirely. Perhaps he meant to do the same – ultimately – to his wife.

Frazee does the same thing. He transports his fiancé's remains from the scene of the crime, it may be that just as Watts transferred the bodies of his children to his truck in plastic containers, Frazee did the same. We know for certain Frazee used an extra-large black plastic tote, but we can only infer that Watts may have. We know the Watts basement was basically filled – floor to ceiling – with containers, and of the right size. But unlike Watts, Frazee added three additional dimensions to his disposal relay.

1. He placed Kelsey's remains out of sight on the top of a haystack for a few days before retrieving it [with the help of an accessory].

2. Instead of oil or acid, Frazee elected to burn Kelsey's remains in an enormous pyre [much as Steven Avery did with <u>Teresa Halbach's remains on Halloween night, in 2005</u>]. And much as Avery lit his bonfire in plain sight right beside his own property, Frazee did the same. Incredibly, there wasn't only one witness to his murderous mischief, but possibly two.

3. The final leg in Frazee's disposal marathon involved scooping up the ashes and transporting them off the property, perhaps to a waste disposal site. Even after this, the burn patch was covered

over, and some of the small artefacts [such as metal fragments] picked up and removed using a magnet.

If the type of disposal was very different, the psychology of the disposal itself is a match, at least in terms of the cruel and sadistic attitude to *completely destroying human remains*, apparently with no compunction in spite of [and perhaps because of] the closeness of the victim to the perpetrator. This closeness adds a taboo aspect to the deed which the perpetrator acknowledges intellectually, and does his damnedest to hide through an elaborate subterfuge. It's in this contrasting sensitivity to the public taboo versus the insensitivity of the deed itself that we intuit a disturbing psychopathy. This psychopathy is less a symptom of criminal psychology, in my view, than a disturbing trend sweeping modern society. Our society today lacks empathy, hence it produces criminals that often show very little remorse or empathy in terms of their victims.

It doesn't seem right, does it? On the one hand our society seems more sensitive than ever to the misdeeds of our fellow man. On the other, although our urgent responsiveness to these misdeeds feels sincere, it's in fact very shallow, very reptilian and very reactionary. We're constantly reacting with self-indignant urgency to dozens, sometimes hundreds of triggering responses each day. One genuine, heartfelt response may be a genuine, heartfelt response. It's difficult to imagine dozens or hundreds a day are all genuine, or heartfelt. Instead, it feels like we are being programmed to be increasingly careless even – and especially – in our most triggered reactions, and we're being triggered constantly. The result? We become numb to others, and even ourselves, ironically through the very process of noticing the things we apparently care about. This programming turns men into machines, and minds into programs. Human beings become algorithms that artificial intelligence is designed to anticipate, game and play – for profit.

If these are the broad strokes connecting not only Frazee to Watts, and Watts to Frazee, but Frazee and Watts to us, and us to them. Are we not so intrigued by the Watts case more than one year on [but as if it were yesterday that we first found out about it] because, somewhere in our hearts and minds that we don't like to acknowledge, we've had similar destructive impulses about "getting rid of" people close to us? Whether in marriages, families, sibling rivalries, isn't this heinous culling of a close and trusted person something millions of people are doing daily – without resorting to murder, naturally, but aren't those nasty impulses there regardless? Isn't that contempt, that sadism, that lack of empathy and remorse creeping increasingly into our psychologies, and thus our communities?

If it is, and I believe it is, then true crime is a sort of "safe pace" where we acknowledge these dark impulses. Just as we deride these perpetrators, we also nod to one another through our participation in the coverage of the crime by saying – yes, this exists. Yes, this is real. If it's real there how real is it here where I am?

Just as criminals and their crimes don't materialize in a vacuum, Criminal Intertextuality[123] [CI] doesn't either. CI predicts a relationship between Watts and Frazee, but more particularly, and more *specifically* between Frazee and Watts. We see this in terrifying technicolor when we examine two simple dates, and examine the linkages between them. Let's do that now, starting with December 5th.

<u>Are you sure you want to hear this?</u>

---

123 <u>True Crime Rocket Science defines Criminal Intertextuality</u> as the tendency of criminals to be influenced by other crimes during premeditation.

1. December 5th – Frazee + Watts

Patricia Key testified about a first-hand encounter with Patrick Frazee on December 5th. As the manager of <u>a credit union branch in Woodland Park</u> [directly <u>across the highway</u> from <u>the Safeway store</u> and <u>just 1.5 miles due south of Kelsey's home</u>], Key was the obvious person for Frazee to deal with. When Frazee entered the compact, standalone credit union building on December 5th, a Wednesday, he told Key he wanted *surveillance photos of himself* from November 22nd, almost two weeks prior. Frazee wanted Key to access the ATM's file footage so that he could *compile a timeline*.

Have you, through the course of your life, ever approached a bank, or store or manager of some branch because you wanted a timeline?[124] Maybe you have but it's not usually associated with innocence. It's often based around legal investigations or nefarious covering up. Frazee's words to Key are also unusual. It's as if he's appropriated them from somewhere else, isn't it? Most of us don't think of our own actions

---

124 CCTV footage has had potential implications for me on two occasions, both were in a gym. In one instance, the brother of an ex-girlfriend claimed I'd purposefully approached him to intimidate him, or physically threaten him. In reality I'd not looked where I was going, and so when I turned I brushed accidentally into the guy. I can't recall if I suggested to the gym manager to refer to the CCTV footage to test his accusation, or whether the gym manager elected to do so on her own. In any event, the CCTV footage convinced the manager that I bore no ill intent. In the other instance a rowdy gym-goer [who was possibly high on drugs] caused a scene in a swimming pool. Two or three people [staff members] were drawn in by this man's strange behavior, including myself. There was a brief verbal exchange, nothing spectacular, followed by more strange behavior that we found out about later, in the changing room. Ultimately the incident was forgotten, and thus the CCTV footage never needed.

as being part of a timeline. Other people tend to think of someone's actions that way.

Frazee is clearly no Chris Watts, because even in his encounter with the bank manager, there's an impression that he talks a lot. In his meeting with Key he went so far as to explain he had broken up with his fiancé the day before he'd drawn money [thus on the 21st] and this preceded a planned discussion – supposedly – on the custody of their child.

Key, testifying as the 8th witness on Trial Day 2, described her encounter with Frazee. According to _9News_:

"That afternoon, I was on the teller line — we were a little short-staffed — and two gentlemen approached me and [specifically] asked if one of my employees was there that day. Once we were in my office, Mr. Frazee asked if he could see the surveillance or video surveillance from our ATM from November 22nd."

The bank manager thought Frazee's interaction with her was weird, but she gave Frazee the benefit of the doubt and handed over a surveillance photo[125] as well as his bank history for November 22nd. The photo showed his red truck as well as Frazee and Kaylee sitting on the front seat of his truck. Frazee also asked for Kelsey's debit card history. Key noted in court that Frazee didn't ask for anything else; no transaction history, photos or video after November 22nd [meaning, he didn't ask because he knew Kelsey was dead and thus there was no additional digital trail to add to his "timeline"].

Interestingly, Key explained to prosecutors that she started off helping Frazee because she initially felt empathetic towards him. But this effort to gain sympathy, to manipulate the manager, was actually

---

125 The ATM surveillance photo hasn't been released to the public to date.

a ruse Frazee was perpetrating to protect himself. Curiously, Key – in coming to Frazee's aid in terms of his timeline – grew suspicious of the timeline he gave her. That's how much he was talking. He seemed to be manufacturing a timeline right there, as if anticipating that Key might be contacted by investigators [as she was] and trying to influence her one way or the other [but she wasn't].

9News quoted some of Key's testimony verbatim:

"What [Frazee] said was: 'All I know was that after [Kelsey] was seen at Safeway, she's talked to her mother on Sunday, and no one's seen her since.' So I stopped the conversation [with Frazee] and said: '[But] if she talked to her mother after Thanksgiving, then [Kelsey] wasn't missing on Thanksgiving.' It was very peculiar to me. [Frazee] was very abrupt. He said: '[Kelsey] didn't talk to her mother on the Sunday after Thanksgiving.' [But] I was thinking: 'You just said that.' It was just a very strange interaction..."

In fact Key was so unnerved by Frazee's mindfuckery, shortly after he left she contacted her company's legal team [they advised her to write a synopsis of the encounter] and then she called the cops. Her synopsis summarized the main points of her conversation with the Florissant rancher. What stood out to her above all? Even within the *schema* of pretending to have broken up with his "still alive" ex, Frazee forgot to pretend to care about Kelsey, or for that matter, Kaylee's well-being.

Key: "The only thing that was really problematic for me in the interaction was there was never any mention of Kelsey..."

Effectively then, Frazee had forgotten to *pretend to act concerned,* or empathetic, within the confines of his own contrivance, his own fiction.

Besides the circumstances and semantics of Key's interaction with Frazee, the real nugget behind her meeting with Kelsey's murderer wasn't so much what was said, or how, but when it was said. The real treasure was the most obvious, the date of the interaction:

December 5, 2018

If True Crime Rocket Science's prediction of Intertextuality [with a capital "I"] is to hold, it means *something from the Watts case had to have crept into Frazee' headspace, infected his psychology, or pinged on his radar either that day or the day prior*. In other words, *something* from the Watts narrative **had to have directly activated Frazee in some way that impacted what he did.** If we can answer the *when* [and we haven't quite done that yet], we need to do so with *what* – we need to identify that *something,* that trigger. The question is was there one, and if there was:

<u>What was it?</u>

<u>What was it!</u>

December 5th was just under two weeks after Chris Watts was sentenced in a Colorado court just 130 miles – as the crow flies – due north of the courthouse in Cripple Creek. December 5th was also just under two weeks after the colossal tranches of discovery – related to the Watts case – were dumped into the public domain. It took the media – and True Crime Rocket Science – several weeks to unpack, analyze and interrogate the voluminous files. But over the course of this period, the media – and True Crime Rocket Science – systematically published[126] some of the most sensational insights extracted fresh from the discovery archives. And December 5th was one of those days.

---

126 In December 2018 *CrimeRocket's* output dipped to 102 from the all-time

Imagine – seriously, put yourself in Frazee's shoes – you're 13 days after committing a murder. You've burned the remains of the victim on your own property. Each time you wake up in the morning and walk out onto the dusty driveway you catch a whiff of burned plastic. Eventually you can't tell if what you're smelling is real, whether it's your memory or your imagination. You're getting jumpy. What do people know? What do they suspect? What are they saying? You monitor the media for any coverage…and that's how you come across <u>a story like this</u>:

How suspicion grew in murder case…Transcript [details] his actions and statements during search for his missing family…

And so <u>you read the story about "how suspicion grew…"</u> Because *you* want to know, in *your* situation, how can *you* mitigate against how suspicion against *you* might grow. Make sense? And so, timeously on December 5th, *The Mercury Times* provided a handy excerpt for a murderer in a similar situation. It was from Coder's August 14th interview with Watts between 19:00 and 23:00. Coder was taking Watts step-by-step through Watts' timeline – <u>his not entirely accurate timeline</u>:

CODER: *Tell me about the call to your day-care.*

WATTS: *To Primrose? I called them to see if the girls were there. They said they weren't there.*

CODER: *Okay.*

WATTS: *I told them since they weren't there [at school], to put them back on the waiting list.*

---

peak of 140 articles [posted in November 2018]. No other month has seen a similar output, since although March 2018 [following the Second Confession and second release of discovery] came closest with 94 posts.

CODER [Breaking in]: *That's not what you told them.*

What's evident here is that Coder knows what's going on as earlier as one day into the investigation. He already has the call records, or if he hasn't, he already has a statement from whoever Watts spoke to at Primrose. And he's using his investigative knowledge to cross-reference Watts to check for signs of deception. And he's caught one. Watts tries to explain himself, tries to dig himself out of the hole he's just fallen into.

WATTS: *I told them [Primrose] that we were gonna sell the house. Um, put it on the market, we probably won't be in the area anymore.*

CODER [Quite rightly]: *That's two different things…*

WATTS [Scrambling]: *Well, I want them to be back on — I put them on the waiting list as they weren't there.*

CODER: *Why weren't they there?*

WATTS: *I don't know.*

CODER: *Where were they gonna go?*

Frazee had to be asking himself, if he was asked, where should he say was Kelsey going to go? And why?

CODER: *Why wouldn't they go to day-care?*

Why wouldn't Kelsey be at work?

It was clear as day that the investigator wasn't buying Watts' story. Frazee had to make sure those investigating his story bought his – hook, line and sinker.

In any event, this was one story that appeared on December 5th. Another appeared *in Inside Edition*. Showing a screengrab from Coonrod's bodycam as he arrived in front of the Watts' home and greeted Nickole Atkinson by hand, the headline reads unambiguously:

HOW SHAN'ANN WATTS' BEST FRIEND HELPED STOP CHRIS WATTS FROM GETTING AWAY WITH MURDER

If you were Patrick Frazee on December 5th, two weeks into your attempt to get away with murder, would this headline catch your attention? Would it send chills down your spine, and make your fingertips spark with adrenalin?

…BEST FRIEND HELPED STOP X…
…FROM GETTING AWAY WITH MURDER…

This story didn't only appear online in the mainstream media coverage, but also appeared on social media, <u>on Facebook with video footage</u>. It was viewed 34 000 times and the footage – now iconic of the Watts case – showed Watts struggling awkwardly as he tried to convince the cops, and Shan'ann's friend, of his story. They weren't convinced. This was an opportunity for Frazee to learn from Watts' mistakes at a very opportune time.

Watts' primary problem was precisely what he told the police: that nobody had heard from his wife, and nobody had seen her. Well, Frazee had taken care of that part. Anything else? The *Inside Edition* reporter in the video <u>says in voiceover narration</u>:

"Because of Nickole, his story is already falling apart…"

And then <u>there's this</u>:

"And this is the moment Watts realizes he was caught on a neighbor's **surveillance camera** *backing his pickup truck into his driveway. Out of the view of the camera, he is loading the three bodies on the truck. Out of Watts' hearing, his neighbor tells police, he is suspicious."*

TRINASTICH: *He looks like he's trying to cover his track.*

"Chris Watts [shown beside the television with his hands on his head] looks like his world is about to collapse..."

You couldn't script a better, more apt, more terror-inducing clip than that to scare the bejesus out of someone facing the exact same set of circumstances – and Frazee was. After seeing this, Frazee's mind raced. What surveillance footage might there be on him? He racked his brain then realized – the ATM. How might he run interference on it? Well, he could imply, infer, suggest and influence the manager [just as Watts tried to interfere with those trying to watch him on the television].

And so, in the afternoon on December 5th, where does Frazee end up going? And what does he end up doing? Checking surveillance footage, and sorting out his timeline so it could be beyond reproach when the cops came calling again…as he knew they would.

But wait, there's more. If you're still not convinced December 5th was CI, how about another date just under a week later?

December 11, 2018

Three weeks after the massive release of discovery, on December 8th details of the digital breadcrumbs relevant to the Watts case continued to slowly filter into the mainstream media. Colorado's _Greeley Tribune_ [which in this case was also syndicated to Moffat County's _Craig Press_] referred to:

Records: Christopher Watts' co-worker went to site, looked for clues day after family's disappearance

In the article an image depicting GPS co-ordinates and an area photo of the well site CERVI 319 provides the exact location of the bodies Watts tried so hard to hide. The caption to the image explicitly states that the data was extracted from the discovery:

GPS tracking data from Christopher Watts' work truck the day he disposed of his wife and kids' bodies.

On December 9th, the *Daily Mail* referred to both Shan'ann's messages to her friends, as well as Kessinger's deleted text messages:

In text message exchanges that were previously revealed, Shan'ann confided in friends that she was worried he did not want their third baby… [Kessinger] told investigators she had deleted texts and photos from Watts out of her phone after learning he was lying, and just wanted him out of her life.

A one-minute video clip in the same story cited Kessinger's internet searches from her phone for wedding dresses "one week before Watts killed his family…"

If the timbre from this trickle of news was steadily unnerving Frazee, and if the general theme was the same [digital data used to track and trace not only messages but *movements*], then the *Daily Mail's* coverage on December 11th was perhaps the final straw.

It was just a few hours after he buried the body of his wife and dumped his daughters in oil tanks that Chris Watts' alibi began to fall apart… That was due in large part to the surveillance footage his neighbor had of Watts on the morning of the murders. That video would later be used to draw out Watts' confession before he was formally charged with murder.

Using reference photos as well as extracts from the discovery, the article goes on to refer to the recovery – in gruesome detail – of the children's bodies. For Frazee this had to be the stuff of his worst nightmares – **remains being recovered from a difficult, hard to locate site in spite of the clandestine efforts that went into hiding them.**

If Frazee was keeping tabs on the goings on surrounding his case, and he certainly was, it's possible the tabloid coverage from Britain's *Daily Mail* didn't blip on his antenna. But <u>*Oxygen's* coverage on December 11</u> surely did. And guess it what it was?

"I can't do this alone with kids..."...messages deal with Shan'ann Watts' anxieties...and provide a snapshot of [troubles within the Watts family].

The first line from the article?

Newly published text messages sent by the wife of convicted killer Chris Watts provide more heart-wrenching details...New texts from the same time period were recently released by the Weld County District Attorney's Office.

Screengrabs of the texts are actually shared in the article, including references to Shan'ann saying:

"I don't want to have this baby."

Virtually the entire article is devoted to how texts extracted from Shan'ann's phone told investigators the real story of what was happening in the Watts marriage.

Frazee had to figure that although Kelsey's remains would likely not be found, the clear and present danger he faced was from **communications surrounding the crime** [communications he *knew* he'd made before, during and after the crime] – with Kenney.

Frazee, studying up on Watts, suddenly felt his own blood turn cold. He had no fucking idea they could get this much from a phone. How could they? Didn't the data belong exclusively to the owner? And was there a way he could scrub it before the cops came knocking again, as Kessinger had partially succeeded in doing? He needed to find out – for his own sanity.

And so, late in the afternoon on Tuesday, just as the stores were closing for the day, Frazee snuck into the squat, square Verizon store just down the road from Safeway.

According to _9News_, Felis testified about the moment he saw Frazee entering the store with one-year-old Kaylee:

"When [Frazee] came in, he seemed very nervous, and kind of sketchy, paranoid and was looking around a lot. One of the first things he said to me was: **'Don't believe what they're saying about me.'** _I said: 'I don't know who you are,_[127] _I treat all my customers the same.'"_

What had gotten Frazee so agitated? Well, besides the gyre of news swilling over Teller County for days following Kelsey's disappearance on Thanksgiving, it was also Frazee's perception of his own prospects based on what had just happened to Chris Watts. In the same way that all of Colorado knew about the Watts case, Frazee felt he was already a marked man too. He was right to be concerned about Felis knowing who he was; Felis _ought_ to have known. But if he could put out a few fires, he might come out of the whole thing a lot better than the Silver Fox from Frederick.

Frazee told Felis he wanted to extract information from a phone he'd previously destroyed. His purpose for access, he explained to the Verizon employee, was _the security_ of the account. You bet it was the security of the account. It was Frazee's _insecurity_ regarding the security of the data.

When Frazee asked the operative question, he gulped heavily. There was a good reason for this gulp. All would be for nought depending on the answer. The Watts case was ample evidence of that. Frazee

---

127 Felis testified that when he identified himself, Frazee's name rang a bell, but he couldn't be sure why.

opened his mouth and thoughts wrote themselves as words. His fate, and Kenney's, seemed suspended as the simple employee absorbed the import of the question.

"If the other phone on my account has been destroyed, can I still access information on it?"

Can I still access it was another way of asking *can anyone else?*

The Verizon employee nodded. Frazee continued to talk, and blink, and gesture. Frazee repeatedly referred not to his active phone, or his active account, but to his "other phone on his account." Now, it's not clear which device – or data – Frazee was targeting. It may have been his own, or Kelsey's or even Kenney's, most likely the latter, purchased by him but given to Kelsey and/or Kenney.

What Frazee seemed to be asking Felis' permission to do was change the PIN on that device because he wanted to access its data. Of course he did. After trawling through the damning data the feds got on Watts, Frazee wanted to wipe the data Verizon had in their digital cloud. Felis said Frazee's request to change the PIN "rang every alarm" in his head.

According to *9News*:

"After [Frazee] asked that question I excused myself to the restroom and looked up the last news report with his name."

What you see here is an Intertextuality *within* a CI scenario. In other words, just as Felis is cottoning on to Frazee's CI, he decides to appraise himself on the context and relationship of what's going on, what's *really* going on, given what he's being asked to do. Felis is doing the right thing, he's educating himself, and so we might refer to this as Civil Intertextuality, which is simply how ordinary people come to know the situation they are in vis-à-vis one another, including potential criminals. It's not quite the same as anybody Googling something out of curiosity, it's within the construct of true crime, but it's where the civilian doesn't have criminal intent, in fact quite the opposite.

When Felis returned from his digital spelunking he let Frazee know there was red tape involved. Without the PIN he wasn't allowed to go into the account [and thus, neither could Frazee]. He'd have to clear the request – Felis told Frazee – through corporate. In other words, Frazee had just found out the same thing that had sunk Watts was likely going to sink him. The answer was no. No, he couldn't alter it or destroy it. No, he couldn't <u>access</u> his phone data. Worst of all:

Yes, someone else could.[128]

If Kelsey was dead, and all traces of her destroyed, digital breadcrumbs remained in the ether, resilient – floating far beyond the reach of Frazee's strong arms, and well beyond the range of all his plots and simple schemes. Yes, beyond such rough instruments as baseball bats and black plastic totes.

If Frazee entered the store shaken, he left stunned, with a tingling sensation rising up his spine and into the hollow center of his brain.

I am so fucking screwed.

---

128 Like his visit to the bank, Frazee's visit to the Verizon store prompted the suspicious staff member to write an email and contact police. If Frazee was trying to pluck as many red flags out of the fabric of his recent misdeeds as he could muster, instead of getting rid of the most significant one, he'd drawn attention to it. He'd just pinned one of the biggest flags to the center of his forehead.

Social Death and Mental Preparation Part 1

The assassination of Jamal Khashoggi...occurred on 2 October 2018 at the Saudi consulate in Istanbul, Turkey... The exact cause of his death is unknown since his body has not been located or examined.
— <u>Wikipedia</u>

A human being is sometimes described as a triad – or a trinity – comprising mind, spirit and body. Each is distinct from the other, but each is in some way related to the other. One cannot have a mind without a body, one can't have a spirit without a body and mind to give life or expression to it. The same triad exists in the vessel of a single true crime case.

A crime is contained in some or other container, and these can be Intertextual too. There may be containers or receptacles for the mind, and for the stuff of the mind, in a crime. For example, information, memory, data needs to be kept somewhere. It resides somewhere, somehow, in some form.

Mental Containers hold personal intangibles like grudges, memories and family dynamics. **Digital Containers** store everything from cell phone records to social media, bank accounts to CCTV footage. Intertextual elements exist within these containers and between them. One can also use certain aspects inside these containers to influence others, or even distort them.

Mental Containers may include a raft of data across a wide spectrum: what grudges existed in the criminal, or his family? How did social death precede real death? It may be harder to access or analyze Mental Containers. Digital Containers may provide clearer clues to issues surrounding mental preparation and/or social death. What do the bank accounts say? Again, how did social death [measured in gold, or in the numbers of full or empty gold cauldrons] precede real death? What does the social media, or the phone records, say about the true identity of the murderer, and the murder victim? How did their respective identities clash, precipitating a social death in terms of one another, and thus fulminating into the incident itself?

If a container exists on the criminal side of equation, it must be precisely duplicated, reproduced, reconstructed or reimagined – mirrored – on the law enforcement and prosecution side. Containers apply to both sides in that each side has the same or similar files, whether real or virtual, whether left at random or assembled, compiled and organized.

Besides Mental and Digital Containers for the paraphernalia that comprises a particular crime or case, there are also **Physical Containers**. To reiterate, this triad of containers in true crime is analogous to the mind, spirit and body of a person.

In this chapter we won't deal with Digital Containers or Physical Containers, nor the Intertextualities between these containers in the

Frazee case and the Watts case.[129] Instead, we'll focus on the Mental Container specifically in the area of Intertextuality. What else informed Frazee's criminal psychology? What moved and inspired him to do what he did, when he did it, and how he did it? You may be thinking we've already addressed this question, and we have – in part.

Strictly speaking, if we stick to the merits of the definition as True Crime Rocket Science defines Criminal Intertextuality, then both the CI's identified in the previous chapter don't apply. They both happened in December. As such they're part of the post-meditation and cover-up, aren't they? True blue CI is specifically about what and how criminals are influenced or inspired to commit their crimes *during premeditation*. It's about the Intertextuality that feeds the crime before it happens. How does it fuel inspiration? Is it all of the inspiration or part of it? So let's go there. Let's go prior to November 22nd and put our true crime filters through the ether. What do you think? If we look do you think we'll find anything there?

<u>Are you sure you want to hear this?</u>

October 2, 2018

<u>At 13:14 on October 2nd</u>, <u>Jamal Khashoggi</u> – a Saudi dissident and journalist for the *Washington Post* – entered the Saudi consulate in Istanbul, Turkey. <u>By 16:00 there was still no sign of Khashoggi</u> even though the consulate officially closed at 15:30. Khashoggi was never seen again, and to the present day, his exact cause of death is unknown.

---

129 The Intertextualities between Digital Containers and Physical Containers in the Watts/Frazee case is covered in *MURDER MOST FOUL MISTRESS ON TRIAL.*

If you were plotting to kill someone circa October 2018 [and Frazee was] and you were attached to this idea of the human remains disappearing forever, therefore "disproving" that a foul deed had ever happened to begin with [AKA "no body no crime"], well then the Khashoggi case was a pretty prescient case study for Frazee, wasn't it?

One of the most compelling aspects – from a criminal's perspective – was the notion that after Khashoggi disappeared, the Saudis didn't feel they owed anyone an explanation. So what if he'd disappeared. Anything could have happened. What did it have to do with them? This made sense to Frazee. So what if Kelsey disappeared? People disappear all the time. Why would it have anything to do with him?

The broader circumstances surrounding Khashoggi's death were captivating for a guy in Frazee's position as well. Khashoggi had gone into the consulate to get papers endorsing his future marriage. His fiancé, Hatice Cengiz, waited outside when Khashoggi entered the consulate. Like Frazee, this was a case that occurred within the cultural context of custody, and the legal frameworks associated with a particular society endorsing a particular social-familial arrangement. For various reasons – some financial, some purely practical – it's occasionally necessary for civilians to get themselves *in the right standing* in the legal sense, in order to be able to function effectively in their various arenas. This was true for Khashoggi just as it was true for Frazee [and to some extent Chris Watts, who faced navigating through the strictures and obligations of a divorce at the time he committed his crime].

If Frazee read about the Khashoggi case, a few things would have resonated [such as his engagement], while other things [like the surveillance footage, and the disposal of remains] would have been instructional. It would be tempting to imagine how the CCTV footage showing Khashoggi going inside the consulate wasn't worth a damn [arguably].[130] What mattered was that no one saw him coming out, a scenario Frazee masterminded as well, if not better than the Saudis.

The Khashoggi case also involved transporting the remains to another location [the Saudi Consul General's residence – at 15:11] for final destruction. It's not known how Khashoggi's remains were destroyed, but it's assumed he was violently and aggressively strangled, dismembered and then once in a safe location under the control [custody] of the right people, his remains were dissolved in acid.

In terms of the aftermath of the Khashoggi murder, a team of cleaners – not quite dressed in Hazmat suits – were also ushered into the scene. They left carrying numerous black bags presumably filled with blood spattered clothing, rags smelling of bleach and other evidence.

On November 5th, 2018 [just over two weeks prior to Kelsey's murder], the *Wall Street Journal* reported on a "clean-up team" dispatched from Saudi Arabia nine days after the murder. Didn't Frazee also have a clean-up team?

As late as October 11 [nine days after the incident] the Saudi's were still maintaining Khashoggi must have left the consulate alive, and since his body was nowhere to be seen, no one could prove anything had happened to him. In the end, Khashoggi's fate was settled by bringing

---

130 In the same way that Khashoggi CCTV evidence wasn't a smoking gun by any means, the Trinastich surveillance footage in the Watts case was damning, but arguably not worth a damn in that it didn't – couldn't – prove anything in a court of law. However, in terms of the overall mosaic, timestamped surveillance footage can be a powerful player in the evidence puzzle, in terms of putting various players at a particular crime scene. In the Frazee case the surveillance footage placed him at the scene, an obvious oversight from him, and perhaps caused by him misapplying the so-called lessons of the Watts and Khashoggi cases as he interpreted them.

in digital evidence. Because the consulate was bugged, Khashoggi could be heard screaming just before he breathed his last.[131]

In sum, the Khashoggi case provided Frazee with a case study on the physical containment of human remains. If Frazee was aware of the Khashoggi case he copied the *modus operandi*. If he wasn't, the *modus operandi* not only of the disposal, but also the execution of the clean-up and attendant plausible deniability, were broadly similar.

August 28, 2018

Less than two months before Kelsey's murder, Frazee's father Robert Edwin died. Besides the legal and financial status of Frazee shifting as a result of this, Frazee would also be practicing how to deal with the death of someone close to him, and measuring how well that sat with him.

In the Watts case, Nut Gate [which invoked the spectre of death around his youngest daughter Ceecee] Watts had a similar opportunity to imagine life without his daughter. Did he really care? He likely decided he didn't. In the Watts case Nut Gate preceded Ceecee's actual death by one month and three days. In the Frazee case his father's death preceded Kelsey's death by two months and three weeks.

August 13, 2018

If Frazee was unaware of the Khashoggi case [which made international headlines for several weeks in October and November 2018], then it's virtually impossible he wasn't aware of Chris Watts, a case that played out in his own neighborhood. In fact the same journalists and

---

131 <u>Khashoggi's last words were</u>:
"Don't do it. You'll suffocate me."

the same publications that directly covered the Watts case, including being physically present in court, also covered the Frazee case. These reporters have since acknowledged how the initial circumstances of the Frazee case immediately resonated with the opening salvos of the Watts case.

The Watts case preceded Frazee's father's death by two weeks and a day, and continued to hog the airwaves non-stop throughout September and October, culminating in the sentencing hearing on November 19th, just three days before Frazee finally yielded to his murderous impulses.

Life After Death – The Phone Narrative

"He wanted to make it look like she was still alive..."
— **Krystal Kenney**

The last known image of Kelsey alive is a surveillance still from November 22nd, timestamped 13:23:48. It's also the last known image of *Frazee with Kelsey*. The fact that Frazee is in this final image is incredibly damning, as well as the dozen or more images where he's visible at Kelsey's door for the next several hours but Kelsey isn't.

If Watts made some clumsy mistakes, leaving evidence in plain sight, this was Frazee's. Frazee may have figured the CCTV image would be lost, especially on a holiday if the resident was elsewhere. He was half right. The video evidence *was* lost. He likely didn't anticipate the higher functions of the Arlo security systems. He may not have known about the continuing screengrabbing and emailing option.

Frazee may also have jumped the gun in his eagerness to commit the crime. He may have seen his scheme to create an elaborate Life After Death would trump any CCTV fragments or footage. And he was right, at least for a few days. When the cops came knocking, all Frazee had to do was hand them his phone and say, "See, she texted me just last week." That was hard to dispute. But when Kelsey remained gone, those texts didn't play so well, especially when the pings and texts stopped, and also *where they were* when they stopped.

Frazee isn't the first to come up with this Life After Death ruse. In the Watts case, the Silver Fox had a weak case that Shan'ann had gotten huffy over his affair and stomped off. Maybe with someone, maybe at her own recognisance. If Watts made one glaring error, it was his failure to get Shan'ann's phone outside of the house. Had Watts simply thrown it out the window of the house or placed it [still on] in a dumpster, there would have been some reason to believe Shan'ann *had* left, or been taken.

One might ask why Watts perhaps wanted Shan'ann's phone. It may be that he wanted to erase information on it, or that he wanted to put information on it. It could also be that he needed her phone to do last-minute banking transfers, and perhaps manage her Thrive.

We've seen Frazee also took an interest in Kelsey's finances after her death. In fact, as has been mentioned earlier, **Frazee made five deposits at an ATM on November 22nd**, along with a single withdrawal.

In the Casey Anthony case, which is highly intertextual[132] in terms of both the Watts and Frazee cases, there's also an elaborate Life After Death fiction, this one involving a fictitious nanny calley Zanny. One could also draw an intertextual line connecting the Anthony case to the Watts case and the Frazee case, and argue that the fictions have become more effective from the one case to the next. Frazee's ruse is undoubtedly the best, and the most convincing of the three. It's tough to say which was more absurd between Casey Anthony's made-up nanny and Watts'

---

132 Frazee told Moore in April 2018 that he'd "figured a way to kill her." April 2018 was the height of the ten-year anniversary coverage of the Casey An-thony case.

virtual, nameless, anonymous friend. Given Watts' more elaborate efforts at concealment [40 miles east of the family home in a secure, access-controlled well site facility], compared to where poor little Caylee was dumped [in the woods a quarter mile from the Anthony home], one tends to lean slightly towards Watts as the "better" criminal. But Casey's social game was better than Watts'. Even if her stories were suspect, Casey's charm and sass gave her the gift of the gab that Watts clearly lacked. It's hard to know whether Frazee had the gift of the gab since we've seen so little of him. In the next narrative in this series that aspect will be dealt with decisively, but it suffices to note here that it does appear Frazee was a convincing liar to those who knew him.[133]

In the Khashoggi case there's a curiously elaborate Life After Death aspect. Mustafa Mohammed al-Madani performed the role of Khashoggi's body double. He left the consulate dressed in Khashoggi's clothing through the back door.[134] The trousers, shirt and jacket were likely still warm when al-Madani put them on. He wore a fake beard as well as Khashoggi's glasses.

The body double made sure he was recorded at the Blue Mosque [a popular tourist attraction] in Istanbul, which would have given people the impression Khashoggi left the consulate [when he hadn't] and that he left the consulate unharmed [when he'd been seriously harmed].

According to *CNN*:

[Khashoggi's] fiancé Hatice Cengiz, who was waiting outside the consulate's front entrance and raised the alarm when he didn't return,

---

133 Patricia Key and David Felis demonstrate how Frazee wasn't a convincing storyteller.

134 The only obvious item of clothing the body double didn't wear was Khashoggi's shoes.

was told by a consulate guard that he may have exited the building through the back door…

What this shows is the vulnerability for Digital Containers to distortions and fictions, just as the spiritual side of people can be preyed on by opportunistic evangelists or sly snake oil salesmen. If Physical and Mental Containers are somewhat resilient, in terms of tampering, or altering, Digital Containers are less so.

In the Khashoggi case the use of the body double shows the perpetrators not only knew about the surveillance cameras [just as Frazee likely knew] but took steps to purposefully control, influence and subvert the digital narrative by infecting it with a deliberate hoax.

This is another compelling intertextuality connecting the circumstances of the Khashoggi case to the Watts case, which is why CrimeRocket covered these similarities in early October, 2018. In that post, the murder of Khashoggi was measured against the concept of a Perfect Murder. As I've emphasized throughout this narrative, if there are more than a few parallels between the Khashoggi case and the Watts case, there's an even closer match with the Frazee case.

The main difference between the fiction of the body double and Frazee's ruse is in Frazee's use of a phone. Kenney essentially played the role of a *digital body double*. She – impersonating Kelsey, and using her phone – sent Frazee texts, which he also responded to.

We will deal with the content, context and timelines of those texts at the end of this chapter, but first let's interrogate how Frazee started to weave his Life After Death narrative, and with whom.

Worth playing for?

#16 HUBER[135]

Besides Kenney, three candidates provided useful intel in court regarding Frazee's Life After Death Ruse. One of these was Frazee's boss, and the other two were cops. Let's start with the cops.

Woodland Park Police Department Corporal Beth Huber joined the investigation into Kelsey's disappearance on December 3rd. It was actually Woodland Park Police Department Corporal Dena Currin who pulled her in. We'll deal with Currin next.

Like Currin, Huber called Kelsey's mother for news and information on Kelsey. According to *The Denver Channel*:

Huber [testified] she learned [Cheryl] had talked with Frazee, who'd said he was talking to Verizon to see if Berreth had texted anyone since she went missing.

The media narrative is somewhat murky regarding the timeline of this call. It likely occurred on December 2nd or 3rd. But we know Frazee only went into Verizon on December 11th. We know he entered the store appearing shaken, and left even more shaken. The next day, December 12th, Jeremy Loew, Frazee's lawyer at the time, told the media his client was cooperating with law enforcement. On December 12th, 2018 *The Denver Channel* noted that Loew had said:

*[Frazee] has provided not only interviews to police, but **has also voluntarily released his phone to be searched by investigators…***

Like Watts' polygraph test, Frazee probably didn't want to release his phone. But he hoped it might exonerate him. Instead, like Watts' terrible polygraph result, it did the opposite.

---

135 Woodland Police Department Corporal Beth Huber was the prosecution's 13th witness.

*"Much has been said over the news and social media about Mr. Frazee's absence at the local news conference recently held by the Woodland Park Police Department on December 10, 2018. Mr. Frazee was first notified of the press conference approximately an hour prior to its commencement. Had he been given more advance notice, he would have participated. [But] Frazee will not speak to the media about this case, as **he does not want to impede the missing person's investigation."***

No, he doesn't want to *impede* the Missing Person's investigation. He wants to help *establish* it. He does want to impede the Missing Person case becoming something else in which someone else – Frazee of course – may be involved.

Now, back to Huber. It was Huber who entered Kelsey as a missing person into the law enforcement systems. Huber also sent through a missing person's alert through the police channels. When Huber sat down with Frazee he said he'd last seen her on Thanksgiving, on the 22nd. They'd spoken the day prior about breaking up. When he went to pick up Kaylee on Thanksgiving, Kelsey wasn't there. [Kaylee wasn't either]. Frazee said he left, ran some errands, and returned later that day. According to Frazee he didn't enter Kelsey's townhome. He simply exchanged Kaylee with Kelsey in the alley.

We can see how Frazee likely anticipated the possibility of some digital evidence, and so his story was taking that into account. But what he didn't know was how much, or how detailed Jackson's footage was.

In Frazee's account to Huber, he said he didn't have any further contact with Kelsey that afternoon, but they did speak later that day and over the course of the next three days.

But <u>cell records</u> would show the last successful outgoing call from Kelsey's phone was at 12:55 on November 22nd. Additional analysis revealed Kelsey's phone travelling west [towards Florissant] with Frazee's phone at the same time – from 16:24 onwards. How could Frazee explain this? That the phones were travelling together?

At 22:22 Frazee's phone was on the move again – and so was Kelsey's – headed to the Nash Ranch. Between 22:48 and 23:08 Kelsey's phone changed direction and headed back to Florissant – with Frazee.

According to _The Denver Channel_:

A few days after Thanksgiving, Frazee received a text from Berreth asking, "Do you even love me?" he told Huber. She said Frazee told her that he tried to reply, but later learned his text didn't go through.

As early as December 3rd, Huber found out from Verizon the last known location of Kelsey's phone. It had pinged off a tower in Gooding, Idaho on November 25th at 17:13. Gooding, Idaho was Frazee's version of Khashoggi's body double floating around the Blue Mosque in Istanbul. It felt out of place and didn't make sense because that's what it was – manufactured evidence.

#17 CURRIN

On December 2nd at 13:50 Woodland Park Police Department Corporal Dena Currin called Patrick Frazee on his cell phone. Moments earlier she'd tried to contact Kelsey and failed to get an answer. Kelsey's mother had given Currin Frazee's contact number.

If Huber's sit down with Frazee was his second encounter with the cops, his fifteen-minute chat with Currin [recorded on Currin's bodycam] was his first.

When the inevitable question came up – when had he last spoken to Kelsey – Frazee had his ruse ready. The last time he'd spoken to Kelsey was the previous Sunday, November 24th.

Sure enough, <u>call records would show the final outbound call from Kelsey's handset at 08:32 on the 24th to Frazee's phone</u>. The call duration was a whopping sixteen minutes and twenty-six seconds. Tough to dispute, right? So what had gone down during this long, and seemingly serious conversation? Since Kelsey wasn't around to give her version, Frazee gave his for her, and that was the point.

They'd talked about how their relationship wasn't working. And Kelsey confided in Frazee that the stress of work was really starting to get at her. It was important to mention work so that the cops knocked on that door next [which they did].

There was some truth to both fictions, of course. For Frazee, certainly, the relationship wasn't working, but <u>revisiting that final image of Frazee with Kelsey</u>, she's carrying a ruby red poinsettia in a flower pot. Had Frazee bought it for her on Thanksgiving as a way to misdirect her, or had she bought it for herself? <u>Kelsey's last text about cooking Frazee a sweet potato casserole</u> [while she was shopping at Safeway] clearly shows her intent, and that at least from her side the relationship was fine, even good.

In the next narrative in this series we'll explore the extent to which Frazee had created the fiction of a bad relationship with Kelsey, along with her being a bad mother – beyond what he told Kenney. The point is Frazee knew there was *some* substance – digital and embedded in the community but both manufactured – to support his yarn to Currin.

There was perhaps more truth to his claim that Kelsey was taking strain at work. A new baby and the hour-long commute would do that to anyone. Of course, if Frazee himself wasn't doing his bit in terms of looking after Kaylee, Kelsey would have taken even more strain. We know that Kelsey had chosen to reduce her work hours, going part-time at Doss Aviation. This also impacted on her benefits, and importantly,

Kaylee's. If Kelsey's employer was no longer covering them, who else would have to?

The Denver Channel describes Frazee telling Currin:

…_he was going to give her space_ for her to figure out what she wanted to do, and if she wanted to find a place in Washington, Idaho or Pueblo.

Naming Washington, Idaho and Pueblo was a nifty bit of dodgerydoo. By invoking three places instead of just Idaho, he knew he was spreading police resources thin on the ground. He was also providing some plausible deniability to the how-should-I-know-where-she-is notion.

During the call, he mentioned that Kelsey had been to rehab for depression and alcohol abuse.[136] _Frazee [also] told Currin he received a text on November 29 that Berreth's phone had expired._

In court, Currin highlighted the same thing everyone else had: Frazee's lack of concern.

#18 SIEBRING[137]

After getting off the line with Frazee, Currin tried Kelsey again, and then – just as she was supposed to – the corporal called Doss Aviation. Frazee's story checked out. Kelsey had sent a text to her boss saying she wouldn't be at work all week because she had gone to see her grandmother. This too is a permutation of Khashoggi going to see the Blue Mosque. It's a strange detail that doesn't quite fit in with a supposedly broken-hearted, overworked mom. It also doesn't quite

---

136 Frazee's "seeding" of the Florissant community with false rumors of Kelsey's alcoholism is part of the subject matter of _MURDER MOST FOUL MISTRESS ON TRIAL._

137 Raymond Siebring, Kelsey's boss, was the prosecution's 4th witness, called to the stand on Trial Day 2.

match the psychology of someone who doesn't care about her daughter, suddenly carrying about her grandmother. Do you see how the pseudo psychology doesn't match up, whereas the sly criminal psychology of Frazee invoking a fictional grandmother feels like the sort of nonsense Frazee would invent?

When Siebring testified he provided some insight into Kelsey's communication style. How did she *typically* text? While not quite as useful as handwriting analysis, on digital platforms different people do have different preferences. Was Siebring able to intuit the difference between the real Kelsey and Frazee's fakery?

Siebring told the court Kelsey was diligent, handled stress well but did occasionally miss work. When she did she always – conscientiously – let the scheduling department know. Prosecutors provided a record of correspondence between Siebring and Kelsey between October and the last day of November.

On November 20th Kelsey texted Siebring to let him know she'd convinced her fiancé to join her at Doss Aviation's holiday party. Once again, this text indicates Kelsey's impression that the relationship was going well as late as two days before her murder. On Thanksgiving Kelsey's boss sent a group text to everyone. Kelsey answered that text late in the day. It read:

"Hi Ray, it was a great day... Happy Thanksgiving to you too."

Siebring thought it was strange Kelsey had used a comma after his name. Typically she used an exclamation mark. Going through her other texts, Siebring noticed something else. Kelsey usually sent smiley faces with her texts. Why wouldn't she on Thanksgiving when she was telling him how great her day was?

Siebring received another text from Kelsey's phone, this one sent by Kenney from Idaho, at 17:06 on November 25th.

"Hi Ray, sorry for the late notice but I won't be able to make it in this week. I need to go see my grandma who is sick..."

Siebring again emphasized the lack of emoticons and exclamation marks. That wasn't as big a clue as the message itself. Why wasn't Kelsey contacting the scheduling department as she usually did? That part was unusual, Siebring admitted. When he tried to contact Kelsey in the days following, with work-related issues there was no answer, which was also telling.

If Frazee had concocted a ruse, it was meant to play out for little more than a week. When Kelsey was supposed to return from her sick grandmother she didn't. When she said she'd call her mother after Thanksgiving, she didn't. When she was supposed to return to work, she didn't.

And so, just as in the Casey Anthony, Chris Watts and Jamal Khashoggi cases, the ruse ran its course for a while. Once it ran out of legs, attention returned to the last time anyone had seen the victims alive. In Frazee's case it came back to the grainy image of Kelsey, Kaylee and the murderer standing at the door. The murderer had his back to the camera but he knew it was there. He reckoned he could defeat the Digital Container with some crafty sleight of hand. But turning one's back on the Digital Container is a serious gamble. Just as committing any crime is a risk for the average criminal, murder is the most dangerous gamble of all. Win, and perhaps something is saved – reputation, a few pots of gold. But taking a life means he stands a chance of losing his life. So committing murder while an eye in the sky is watching *and doing it anyway* is as high stakes as it gets.[138]

---

138 The Saudis, Watts and Frazee all took on the surveillance cameras and all lost. One possible case <u>where surveillance cameras may have been successfully used</u> by suspects is the Rebecca Zahau case.

VERDICT

"Maybe I would be better off dead." — Kelsey Berreth [according to Patrick Frazee, following an argument the couple had in 2017]

~

"Proof of being an idiot..."

"Never argue with an idiot. They will drag you down to their level and beat you with experience."
— Mark Twain

At the beginning of the trial Frazee's defense compared opposing counsel's case to a beautiful house with serious foundation issues. From the outside, their analogy went, the case looks good and solid. But check the corners, nooks and crannies, analyze the evidence, look closer at the details, examine the evidence and "the jury will see deep issues."

Instead the jury – as we know – saw deep issues with the "beautiful house" that started off as Frazee himself, and Frazee's story. Just as Kelsey [and Kenney, and others] saw Frazee as the handsome cowboy, it turned out that whole identity [much like Watts, much like so many other criminals] was an identity built on cards. The hero was a gleaming fake. His hero identity was a house built on cards. Look closer and that identity falls apart. Why? Maybe there's no man behind the money, and maybe it's because there's no money. Maybe the man has mommy issues. Maybe the man, strong and charismatic as he seems, isn't a real man after all.

Ashley Porter, in her opening arguments on the first day, described the prosecution's case as "a raw and unedited version." Nice mindfuckery there. It's a mental nod to the glitches that are invariably present in the Digital Container. Digital evidence is sometimes very strong, often as incontestable as DNA. But just as frequently it's neither here nor there. It's fuzzy. It's an incomplete specimen. And Jackson's footage was a lot like that. Porter wanted the jury to throw out this evidence because it wasn't 100% clear cut.

PORTER: *All of these facts that don't make sense. All of these facts actually support Patrick Frazee not being [responsible for] the disappearance of Kelsey Berreth.*

An important point made by Porter was that Frazee was seen entering and leaving Kelsey's townhome *in the same outfit*. If there was a bloodbath, how was that possible? *He'd* not brought a hazmat suit or plastic booties with him. And if there was a bloodbath, and there was, how come there was no blood on him?

Porter pointed out that since Kelsey was still missing, she was still considered a missing person. There was no murder weapon, and no witnesses from the day of the "alleged" crime had come forward. Besides all that, there was no clear motive. Frazee had maintained his innocence throughout [just not testified himself, nor fielded any kind of defense besides edits, excuses and interruptions to the prosecution's case][139] and been co-operative with law enforcement. Kenney had been the one with burner phones, burning bodies, covering up and telling lies. Look at *her* – was the defenses message – not him.

By the end of the trial, Frazee's defense was still more or less on the same track.

---

139 An ironic legal mirror to the defense assertion that the prosecution's case as vraw and unedited, was the failure by Frazee's defense to even field a defense.

Closing Arguments

#1 DEFENSE[140]

If Porter led the opening for the defense case, Steigerwald handled the closing arguments. Kenney was an unreliable witness who was saying whatever she could to protect herself. Frazee didn't kill Kelsey. What's more, the prosecution had built their entire case on the foundations of an unreliable timeline which they got from an unreliable mistress.[141]

Steigerwald emphasized how Kenney's timeline was "made up", manufactured to fit the prosecution's case. The unreliable timeline thing is interesting given the elaborate fiction of the phone, and the *Life After Death* ruse, isn't it? All those moments and messages, the movements to Gooding, the messages about "Do you still love me?" were all *made up* to set up a brand new house of cards – this notion that Kelsey was alive and kicking, and that Kelsey's Ghost had a different attitude to their relationship, and to custody.

One house of cards is hidden by the distraction of another. Attack is the best form of defense sometimes, and so instead of defending Frazee's timeline, it was easier – or simpler – to simply attack, undermine and question the prosecution's timeline.

---

140 The protocol in court in criminal trials is for the prosecution to close first. For reasons of narrative efficacy, the defense closing is provided first in this instance.

141 Was Kenney an unreliable mistress? It seems Frazee leaned on her pretty heavily. Did she deliver to his specifications? In terms of cleaning up his "mess" she absolutely did. In this sense she was a reliable "accessory", so why can she not be considered a reliable witness once her priorities and loyalties were with the prosecution's case?

STEIGERWALD: *You are being asked to ignore your common sense and the direct evidence that has been presented to you the last two-plus weeks, and to listen to the circumstantial evidence that supports [Kelsey's story].*

The Frazee case certainly is a circumstantial evidence case. Unfortunately for Frazee, the circumstantial mosaic turned out to be very detailed, and as a result, very compelling. A strong circumstantial-evidence case – surprise, surprise – *is* sufficient to convict even without a body. Frazee may have assumed the opposite from watching one too-many television shows. Watching <u>a Hollywood movie about murder with a dramatized court narrative</u> may be convincing on a particular legal point, but it's not necessarily the law.

Steigerwald, presumably with a straight face, told the jury if one detail in the timeline was wrong, the whole thing [the whole house, the whole case in this case] comes crashing down. For Steigerwald the weakness in the prosecution's case was the surveillance footage. Where's the black tote? Where's the bat Frazee was supposed to be carrying? Where is Frazee seen anywhere carrying, or moving the tote? How did anyone know for sure Kelsey was is it? Nobody did!

Why is there no blood on Frazee's clothing? Why was there none in Kelsey's washing machine?[142] Perhaps the strongest argument led by Frazee's defense was similar to the defenses employed by Amanda Knox's lawyer and Casey Anthony's in their respective trials. It's the notion that all of the weird shit surrounding an incident can be explained by the prime suspect being a little strange. Maybe my client is goofy, maybe my client is a habitual liar. Maybe my client frequently

---

142 It's interesting that the defense actually led the argument about the washing machine in the townhome. One way to clean bloody clothes, of course, is to wash them.

cons people and systematically deceives many different people. That doesn't make him/her a murderer. Well, *it often does.*

According to Steigerwald, Frazee's plan to kill Kelsey on Thanksgiving was "the worst plan" because:

1. *"There are few other days when someone is less likely to be alone than on a major holiday like Thanksgiving."*

2. *"Neighbors were more likely to be home on Thanksgiving."*

3. *"The kitchen window blinds were open for 48 hours after the murder. Why didn't anyone see anything?"*

4. *"If Frazee wanted to kill Kelsey, why didn't he just do it in the middle of nowhere, either in Florissant or on the Nash Ranch?"*

These are excellent points. Keep them in your psychological back pocket. We'll address them in the final chapter.

Steigerwald still wasn't done. Flicking his hands towards the prosecution, he asked why opposing counsel hadn't tried to burn the black tote themselves. Why not burn the same tote in the same way [as described] and prove it melted down in the same way Frazee's inferno supposedly did. Steigerwald said prosecutors didn't do it because *they didn't want to know the answer.* This question is worth addressing here, briefly.

Firstly, the defense were free to do the same, to *disprove* their client's culpability, and yet why hadn't they done so? **Secondly,** the burn patch, the burnt plastic smell and the evidence of three witnesses[143] confirmed the same thing – not just a fire but the location and specific

---

143 The three witnesses confirming that a burn had in fact occurred were Kenney and the two ranch hands.

details surrounding it. A fourth witness[144] also highlighted the most compelling aspect of all – the human tooth fragment belonging to a female. **Thirdly,** had the prosecution indeed demonstrated the incineration of a tote, *any* discrepancy could be used to attempt to infer reasonable doubt.[145]

Next Steigerwald dealt with the cadaver dogs. Only three items elicited interest from the dogs. Kelsey's underwear found in her townhome. The rear bumper of the Toyota Corolla [a vehicle owned by both Kelsey and Frazee]. The third indication occurred on the top of the hay bale inside the red barn on the Nash Ranch. Steigerwald said Hurst's bloodhound Radar didn't smell anything. The dog was simply nervous and unsteady on such an uneven, and unstable surface and chose to sit down [sitting was Radar's way of alerting]. This wasn't a bad argument from Steigerwald. Radar's "indication" isn't particularly convincing. So there's likely some truth to Steigerwald psyche evaluation on the dog.

Even if there is, the odds are the tote was temporarily stored in the barn, and there were traces of human decomposition in the hay inside that barn. The stains may have been gasoline or oil or bleach used to destroy other stains, but the fact that stains were where Kenney said they'd be was chilling.

---

144 Diane France analyzed the tooth fragment recovered from the burn patch.

145 Interestingly, in the Oscar Pistorius case, Oscar claimed the loud shrieks and screams before several shots were not from the victim – Reeva Steenkamp. It was not Reeva's petrified screams it was his. And the shots the neighbors heard, Oscar claimed, weren't shots but him trying to smash down the door. The defense demonstrated loud bangs on a door with a bat. While there was some doubt that these bangs sounded like shots, one thing the defense never did was have Oscar "scream like a woman" [as he'd claimed] in court. Nevertheless, throughout his testimony Oscar spoke in a high-pitched voice that was different to the way he sounded in numerous television interviews.

In terms of direct evidence, the defense had a strong case. And this had been Frazee's defense all along. The whole idea was for there to be no direct evidence, and he thought this would suffice.

NO BODY = NO CRIME.

NONE OF MY DNA = I DIDN'T DO IT

LIFE AFTER DEATH DATA = PLAUSIBLE DENIABILITY

While all of this makes sense on paper, the legal process is – fortunately – not quite as simple. Criminal law makes room for subtlety and nuance, even if it expects proof beyond reasonable doubt. And circumstantial evidence is proof.

Steigerwald – like Amanda Knox, like Steven Avery, like OJ, like Damien Echols – repeats the familiar claim that if one's DNA isn't somewhere, it means the suspect wasn't there. It's a clever argument. It feels like a smoking gun.

NO DNA = I WASN'T THERE

And yet Frazee was there. The surveillance camera screengrabs show he was there. Kelsey was his fiancé, so one would expect him to be there, and for traces of him to be there. The fact that his DNA isn't there is what's really weird. Why isn't it there? Why is so little DNA of *anyone* in the house?

In his closing, Steigerwald asked a rhetorical question. Why would Frazee tell so many people he wanted to kill Kelsey?[146] Well, one reason is because that's what he wanted to do. He said what was on

---

146 The answer to the question of why Frazee told so many people about Kelsey is explored in-depth in *MURDERMOST FOUL MISTRESS OF TRIAL.*

his mind. <u>Didn't OJ do the same before Nicole Brown was murdered?</u> <u>Didn't Steven Avery do the same thing?</u> There's also an allegation that someone expressed the intention to kill Rebecca Zahau – <u>or Zahau feared someone might</u> – after the child in her care fell down the stairs in the Spreckels Mansion. And <u>Damien Echols</u>?

According to Steigerwald, saying he wanted to kill someone, and then a witness coming forward to say that he had, and the victim disappearing permanently didn't mean anything. Where was the evidence? Use your common sense. Well yes, the jury were about to.

A Bittersweet Day

"It's clear we don't want him to know the facts of the case." — Fourth Judicial District Attorney Dan May

In a slap towards opposing counsel, Steigerwald said there was too much attention during the trial on "the stupid things" Frazee told other people. One of those stupid things was said on December 20th, to Joseph Moore:

"If I'd known it would have blown up this big, I never would have —"

If Frazee was taking his cues from the Watts case, either he missed the way that story gained traction, or perhaps he thought the furore around the Watts case [a triple murder] would drown out a disappearance in a small rural community in Nowhere, Colorado. It wasn't a bad line of reasoning, if that's what it was. But if that's what it was, Frazee failed to take his own intertextuality further as well. If he was using the lessons of the Watts case, why wouldn't someone else? Like the media? Like the occasional True Crime Rocket Scientist?

Steigerwald rationalized the "stupid statements" his client made by invoking the loss of Frazee's father, and an ongoing battle between Frazee and his siblings over his inheritance. Steigerwald emphasized his poor client was sort of an outcast with no one to give him advice. There was *no one* the poor <u>schmo</u> could trust. Oh, no one like Sheila – whom he'd been living with for 20 years or more?

And as for what Frazee had said to the snitch, Steigerwald didn't see anything wrong with asking someone to kill a bunch of people. People freak out all the time, and this was just Frazee's way of freaking out [making hit lists and planning murders].

Referring to Frazee's s scribbles and correspondence that collectively we might refer to as the Toilet Paper Trail [TPT], Steigerwald concluded:

"That's not proof of anything. That's only proof of being an idiot. Not proof of him doing anything."

Do you see how the defense play their case? Where there's circumstantial evidence it's not real, it's raw and unedited. Where there's direct evidence implicating Frazee in murderous schemes and plots, that's not real either, it's just proof of Frazee being an idiot, and freaking out.

Steigerwald finished the defense case by reminding the jury how shaky the foundation of the house was, and that the whole thing [the prosecution's case] comes crashing down because of it.

"If you have [any] hesitation, it's because Frazee is not guilty."

It was up to Beth Reed from the prosecution to invert Steigerwald's story. Reed had to show the jury, in her closing, that Frazee being an idiot *was* proof that he was a murderer. It wasn't a hard case to sell.

#2 PROSECUTION CLOSING[147]

Reed started by showing the court a photograph of Kelsey. It showed Kelsey's date of birth, and explicitly indicated her death, and

---

147 As noted earlier, the protocol in criminal trials is for the prosecution to field their closing arguments first. For reasons of narrative efficacy, the prosecution's closing – including their rebuttal arguments – are provided second in this instance.

the date of her death. Reed empathized with Kelsey, and with the plight of the jury, saying:

"We all wish Kelsey had walked through that door, right now…"

This practical demonstration of the jury's dilemma was brilliant in its simplicity. If Kelsey's alive, where is she? She's not here because she's not alive. That was an excellent argument to open up with. It was also an easy one to go along with. Next, Reed emphasized another "stupid thing" Frazee had said.

According to <u>The Denver Channel</u>:

[Reed] *said when it was suggested that [Kelsey] could come back by Joe Moore, Frazee replied, "That's never going to happen."[Then Reed] walked…jurors…through the past two weeks of testimony [where] witnesses outlined months of alleged plotting by Frazee to kill [Kelsey]… Reed told the court that Frazee knew [Kelsey] was dead when he said multiple times in December 2018 that [she] was not coming back. [Frazee] knew [Kelsey] was dead when he went to a credit union and Verizon store to try to establish alibis…*

At the Verizon store Frazee said another stupid thing:

"What happens to a destroyed, damaged or lost phone? Can you recover information?"

Reed said Frazee knew Kelsey was dead because after November 25th, the ruse ran out of steam.

"There was zero communication after that…"

The reason for this is because Kelsey's phone had been destroyed. Next Reed dealt with Kelsey's intentionality. Did her behavior before her disappearance match the impression of a depressed, dysfunctional or reckless individual? Reed referred to Kelsey getting medication in the middle of night for her sick fiancé. Showing the jury a Safeway receipt and the sheer amount of groceries Kelsey bought on November 22nd [a nice, intuitive touch], Reed said this wasn't indicative of someone about to walk out on her child, and fiancé.

"While Kelsey is planning [her] future, this man is planning to kill her for months."

Moreover, video evidence proved Frazee wasn't checking on cows, or watering his horses on Thanksgiving afternoon. Where was he? He was at Kelsey's townhome, killing her, while Kaylee listened from a back room.

According to *The Denver Channel*, besides the surveillance footage:

Reed pointed out that [Frazee's] phone was utilizing the Woodland Park cell phone tower…[And]…later that afternoon, just before 17:00, Frazee's truck was seen on a camera and that black tote in the back of his truck had changed positions. **"Because Kelsey Berreth is in that box," Reed said.**

#3 REBUTALL

In the final salvo of the trial from either counsel, District Attorney Dan May stood up to rebut a few aspects from Frazee's defense.

May pointed out how Frazee had "trashed" Kelsey's reputation for a long time before she disappeared. If the jury had been thrown a curveball by the defenses claim of there being no "direct evidence", May set them straight. Kenney's testimony – all of it – was direct evidence. She was the witness to the crime. It was tougher to get more direct than someone directing investigators to evidence she'd been directed to by the murderer to clean up. Once again, the defense saying "there's no direct evidence" isn't the same as "our case is that there's no direct evidence."[148]

---

148 In several of <u>Amanda Knox's media interviews she repeats the claim that</u>

May called Kenney's cleaning of the crime scene, taking the tote from the barn and burning it all examples of direct evidence. In terms of the timeline, May countered that Frazee's story didn't match the digital tracking undertaken by law enforcement, while Kenney's story did.

May also provided a nifty counter to the absence of Frazee's DNA at the crime scene – *Kenney's was also absent.*

Perhaps May's strongest statement, and possibly the strongest statement of the 11-day trial, was this one, cited by *The Denver Channel*:

He took a bat into Kelsey's apartment and he beat her, and he beat her, and he beat her, and he beat her. And at some point in that, the victim said, 'Please stop.'" [Now] we want to hold him accountable. **We are asking you to please stop this defendant from getting away with murder,** *and find him guilty on all charges."*

At 11:08 on Trial Day 11 a murder case comprising more than 70 prosecution witnesses, over 600 evidence items and thousands of pages of discovery, was handed over to the jury. At 14:45, after three-and-a-half hours of deliberations the jury did exactly as May had asked. As Kelsey's father glared at the Florissant cowboy, <u>Frazee was found guilty on all charges and sentenced to the maximum – life without parole plus 156 years</u>. Frazee didn't react when he heard his fate. Steigerwald shook his head.

No body, it turns out, *was* a crime, and in this case, a very serious one.

<u>there is no direct evidence of herself at the crime scene</u>. More accurately, the direct DNA evidence that was discovered implicating Knox was successfully disputed, and the crime scene referred to was the inside of Meredith Kercher's room, not the outside. <u>This argument is very different from an absolute claim that "there is no evidence of me at the crime scene."</u>

Murder Most Foul

"People aren't easy to kill. They're very resilient. And beatings are nasty in that they don't really have the effect that they have on television."
— Jonathyn Priest, Crime Scene Analyst

[WARNING: GRAPHIC CONTENT]

After the verdict, Judge Sells told Frazee to stand up. To his face, Judge Sells called Frazee's actions vicious, senseless and without reason.

"Kelsey spent her last night caring for you," Sells intoned, "and you repaid that kindness in the morning by viciously beating her to death. Your crimes deserve the absolute maximum punishment and I intend to do that."

That was the worst the Judge could inflict on Frazee – harsh words, and a lifetime to ponder them. Frazee, meanwhile, had rendered much harsher punishment on his victim. An incredibly cruel barrage of devastating blows, which after a few minutes deprived her of decades of sweet living, and deprived her infant daughter of a mother, and a mother's relationship with her first child.

In the *Rocket Science* narratives, the reader is often presented with an ominous sounding choice:

Are you sure you want to hear this?

And often, you do.

In this chapter, this question for this narrative will be posed a final time. It's not meant rhetorically, and the reader needs to think carefully and soberly if you *do* really want to hear this.[149]

Speaking on the *CBS* documentary which aired following the verdict, Dan May emphasized that the jury needed to hear[150] what happened to Kelsey in order to sentence her murderer appropriately. In true crime, our search for the truth must be the same, even where that truth is cold, hard and unbearable to look at.[151] Quiet, sweet and kind as Kelsey was, described by those who loved her as "a light" of the world, probably she – like Jesus – if she could have walked into the

---

149 I've had to do some soul-searching on whether Kelsey's murder – given its gratuitous nature – ought to be reconstructed at all. Reconstructions are essential to true crime, to the analysis and the fabric of presenting an argument. As such, the reconstruction of Kelsey's murder was essential to the prosecution's case. But is it really essential to this narrative?

150 Citing what he'd said to the jury during his rebuttal, Dan May explained to *CBS* why the jury need to know the exact details of what Kelsey went through in her final moments:
"He keeps, beating her, and beating her, and beating her. … The jury needed to hear that, they needed to hear how brutal this was, how uncaring he was. How senseless this was."

151 Jennifer Viehman told the media after the verdict:
"It was hard. It's heart-breaking, because we know what her last moments on this Earth were like…It's heart-breaking, because we know what happened to her."

court, may have said, 'Look at my wounds, look at what he did to me. Look.'

Should you look, or should you look away? And so:

Are you sure you want to hear this?

Let us begin by removing those four questions raised earlier from the back-pocket.

1. "There are few other days when someone is less likely to be alone than on a major holiday like Thanksgiving."

But Kelsey would be alone – with him.

And Frazee thought he might be able to rely on his family covering for him. Where were you on Thanksgiving? With my family of course.

Besides that, police resources and the vigilance of the community would be inner-directed and distracted, allowing him to come and go without people necessarily noticing.

2. "Neighbors were more likely to be home on Thanksgiving."

Kelsey's weren't, and one suspects Frazee found out about this in advance.

3. "The kitchen window blinds[152] were open for 48 hours after the murder. Why didn't anyone see anything?"

Frazee may have covered up the obvious mess seen through the window with a few wipes. The kitchen window looked out onto a private walkway that no one used except Kelsey, and provided a limited view of the interior to the lounge. In order to see into the lounge area, one would need to move to one side outside, but even the kitchen cabinets

---

152 The kitchen window is covered over during Kenney's walk-through by a white and pink towel.

and stove would obscure the view of the floor and to some extent the walls.

4. "If Frazee wanted to kill Kelsey, why didn't he just do it in the middle of nowhere, either in Florissant or on the Nash Ranch?"

Frazee didn't kill Kelsey on his property as he felt that would implicate him. For some reason he didn't think disposing of her body on his property was risky, perhaps because of the size of his property, and his unique knowledge of the resources he knew he had available and had perhaps used in the past to get rid of dead animals.

<u>Which brings us at last to the moment of truth.</u>

Patrick Frazee is with his mother, brother and the children eating dessert on the Ranch. He lifts a scoop of sweet stuff to his mouth. It's a weird sensation doing something so normal, after what he's done. He's half-relaxed, and half-antsy, half-participating in the conversation with his brother's wife, and half-somewhere.

He scoops another spoonful and gulps it down. Then glances at the television. Zooming into his green rancher's eyes, into his mind's eye, another room, another setting, from another time, emerges. He drifts out of time back to those visceral moments. He will revisit them countless times, but this, so far, is the first.

"What are you doing?" It's Kelsey's voice. Soft. Kind. Conscientious.

"I'm putting Kaylee in the chair. [Chuckles]. Take it easy babe, [pushing her back] there's something I want to show you."

"What?"

Kelsey retreats, good-naturedly. The rancher shepherds her through the kitchen, to the center of the lounge.

"But...[motioning to Kaylee].

"No, Kels, in the lounge….trust me, this will just take a second. How good are you at scents?"

"Pretty good. What is going on?"

"Pretty good eh? Let's see. Put this on."

"Can't I just close my eyes?"

"Put this on."

Kelsey puts the sweater over her face. Frazee glances furtively at the door, scoots over to pull the door closed,[153] *and snaps up a baseball bat stowed right behind the door. He glances quickly at the windows.*

"No peeking. Promise me – no peeking."

"I won't peek. Where are the candles?"

"Just plugging one in right now. Give me a second. Stand still."

He draws a curtain. A shadow falls over the inside of the condo, and over Kelsey.

"Why—s"

Frazee places the bat an inch from the back of her head. He aims. Then his grey-green eyes darken. Her head, covered in a sweater, has no idea what's happening around her. Frazee's successfully tricked her, but the trick has been a long time coming, and he's just getting started.

In an instant he has a last thought, on her behalf:

I've waited a long time for this. *[Does he say it? Does he taunt her, or just think it?]*

---

153 It's conceivable that Frazee may have left the door open. On the other hand, he may have closed it to prevent Kaylee from seeing her mother in distress and her crying as a result.

You're in the way.

And I can't afford you – or this – anymore.

It's just become too expensive…so…

SWING AWAY.

<u>*BFF.*</u>

The bat smashes Kelsey full on the back of her head. Her hands shoot outward in shock, some loose hair flicks into a brief brown star as she stumbles forward. Just after she makes her muffled landing on the wooden floor on all fours, Frazee lands another enormous blow.

CRRKKK.

Kelsey coughs, involuntarily. Adrenalin activates her thin frame. The instinct to survive kicks in.

BFFGH.

Realizing now what's happening to her, Kelsey tries to crawl, wriggle, kick. She swings an arm defensively, while another scratches at the floor, at his trouser leg.

DFWWW

The fourth blow is deflected slightly by a flailing arm. Kelsey tries to stand. Frazee moves, guarding the exit, but Kelsey moves too. Frazee smashes at the offending arm, breaking it.

<u>*You wanna play? Huh?*</u>

Now her arms are limp at her side. She's broken, defeated, defenseless. Her feet wobble; she sways slightly, unsteadily. The sixth blow to her stomach winds her. He uses the head of the bat and pummels it into her midriff. She sinks to her knees, letting out a sputtering sob. Before she can catch her breath, before she can say anything, another blow pummelling the jutting wing of slim shoulder, breaking it.

BFFFF.

"Pleassse…" It's a weak, hissy sound, like the sound of baby bird.

"Ssstop."

Frazee scampers towards her feet and rains another brutal blow into the small of her back, just below the neck.

The seventh blow is to her face. She teeters over, face down, to the floor. It's around this time that Frazee notices the blood for the first time. On his hand, on the bat. He needs more blood. He needs to get this over and done with.

Now, <u>with each successive blow an arc of blood rains onto the wall</u>. Frazee can't understand how she's still alive, still moving. With as much might as he can muster, he smashes two, three more times. Each blow crunches bone, breaks teeth.

Now he's gasping with the effort, grinning through a mask of red blood. Frazee steps back, skids on the blood, the whites of his eyes vivid in the gloom. There's so much blood on the floor. He glances to the door. Then down to the floor. She's still moving. Her fingers tremble with pain and shock. One foot quivers as nerves struggle to maintain tenuous lines of control. He lands a blow, swings back [casting blood behind him] and pounds the limp form again.

Frazee needs another breather.

He glances around again.

Listening.

Electricity is buzzing through his shoulders. He hears the faintest sputtering noise. Another blow.

Then another.

Finally he moves alongside her prostrated, bloodied form. He has plenty of time now. He slips slightly in the pool of blood again, then steps around to the floor where there is no slick. She's not moving, but he has to make sure.

He places the nose of the bat where he'd first placed it, raises it slowly and lands the last blow.

BBBFFFT.

His dark eyes dance around him, his pink face fired up with effort and sprayed with her blood.

"There was blood splattered on the east wall, taller than me. There was splatter, on stuffed animals, an exercise ball, a cedar chest. It was on the west wall, on the sink, the stove, on the dishwasher. The majority was on the hardwood floor in the living room."[154]

A spoon CLINKING into a plate brings Frazee back to the present. The ranch. A rag doll of bloodied pulp, matted hair, brain and bone fragments is in the black box in the bed of his red truck. He's brought her here while he has Thanksgiving dinner with his family. He's intrigued by how much he's unnerved by the situation. She's not going anywhere, but her stuff is leaking out everywhere. He needs to get rid of it, put it somewhere else.

Two days later Kenney is standing in the same room. She finds a sweater on the floor, black with blood. After finishing their burgers from Sonic, Kenney – according to _ABC_ - asked Frazee about the murder.

---

154 The bold text is from Krystal Kenney's testimony.

Frazee told [Kenney] he "swung away" but called the method "inhumane" and said in the future he would stick to "normal weapons." She said that he told her he brought a tote in from the back of the truck after he killed Berreth and put the bat inside, then washed his pants and tried cleaning up.

The handsome rancher from Florissant – unlike Chris Watts - was never very good at cleaning up after himself. This murder, this *murder most foul* was a mess too vast for any one person to make disappear. Even for two people working in concert, the cosmic scale of this crime would not remain hidden from the world.

About the Author

Nick van der Leek [*True Crime Rocket Science* on YouTube, *@CrimeRocket* on Twitter and *@Nickvdk* on Instagram] *is a widely published photojournalist and the author of 100 books, including several trilogies dedicated to unravelling the world famous, and still officially unsolved JonBenét Ramsey and Madeleine McCann cases.*

Instead of journalism, Van der Leek studied law, economics and marketing. After two years cutting his teeth in a busy newsroom he became a full-time investigative writer. Today he is one of the most prolific true crime authors in the world.

He has sat in on many high-profile court cases, including Oscar Pistorius, Henri van Breda and Jason Rohde, and has occasionally advised criminal prosecutors during court cases on an extemporary basis. His research on the mysterious death of Vincent van Gogh has been added to the archives of the Van Gogh Library, in Nuenen, the Netherlands.

The next Rocket Science title, SILVER FOX II, reveals additional insights into this fascinating case. Available early 2020.

For more information on new releases, reviews, blogs and discussions, visit crimerocket.com. Join the True Crime Rocket Science Community on Patreon at https://www.patreon.com/TCRS.